A POSITIVE VIEW OF LGBTQ

Embracing Identity and Cultivating Well-Being

Ellen D. B. Riggle and Sharon S. Rostosky

ROWMAN & LITTLEFIELD
Lanham • Boulder • New York • Toronto • Plymouth, UK

Published by Rowman & Littlefield
4501 Forbes Boulevard, Suite 200, Lanham, Maryland 20706
www.rowman.com

10 Thornbury Road, Plymouth PL6 7PP, United Kingdom

British Library Cataloguing in Publication Information Available

Library of Congress Cataloging-in-Publication Data

The hardback edition of this book was previously cataloged by the Library of
Congress as follows:

Riggle, Ellen D. B.
    A positive view of LGBTQ : embracing identity and cultivating well-being /
Ellen D.B. Riggle and Sharon S. Rostosky.
        p. cm.
    Includes bibliographical references and index.
    1. Sexual minorities. 2. Gender identity. 3. Positive psychology. I.
Rostosky, Sharon Scales II. Title.
    HQ73.R54 2012
    155.3'3—dc23
                                                                    2011027007
ISBN: 978-1-4422-1281-7 (cloth : alk. paper)
ISBN: 978-1-4422-1282-4 (pbk. : alk. paper)
ISBN: 978-1-4422-1283-1 (electronic)

Printed in the United States of America

To Brett, Rea, and Matthew
You inspire us!

CONTENTS

ACKNOWLEDGMENTS

We have become convinced during this process that it takes a village to write a book! We are grateful for the support of many people.

The first person we would like to thank is Sue Strong. Sue is the person who asked the original question, "What's positive about being a lesbian?" What started as a question among friends eventually became the focus of a national survey for the LGBTQ community. We appreciate that she had the insight to ask an important question. She has that knack.

We thank our coauthors on the original journal articles for their insights into the analysis of the data for those articles. Joy Whitman, Amber Olson, and Sue Strong worked with us to analyze the samples of gay men and lesbians. David Pascale-Hague and LaWanda McCants worked with us to analyze the samples of bisexual- and transgender-identified participants. We appreciate their insights and thank them for the role that they played in this project.

We appreciate the technical support of C. Stuart Reedy. In our humble opinion, Stu is a magician. He has worked with us for countless hours on several projects and is always there making things work for our online surveys. Thank you, Stu!

Jan Oaks took on the task of trying to teach us to write without using nearly indecipherable jargon and long run-on sentences. All of the remaining jargon, run-on sentences, and other bad writing habits are our responsibility. We also appreciate the insightful comments of K. J. Rawson. We appreciate the work of Jennifer Cook in helping create a list of resources for this book. Many other friends and colleagues provided encouragement along this journey. We appreciate their support.

We extend our special thanks to Glenda Russell and Janis Bohan. These two looked at us on numerous occasions and asked us point-blank when we were going to write this book. They were very impatient. And very supportive. They read chapters and provided feedback in the most thoughtful, kind, and supportive manner imaginable.

We would like to thank Anne and Liz for our "writer's retreat." And, of course, Zener, who kept us company and entertained us as we worked (we'll thank Tillie too, although she spent most of the time hiding from us under the bed). As we have joked, we know that it is "sooo lesbian" to thank cats in the acknowledgments!

We thank Suzanne Staszak-Silva, our editor at Rowman & Littlefield. We appreciate her support and feedback.

We owe a big debt of gratitude to all those who have participated in our online surveys and interviews over the past decade (plus). Obviously, these are the people who have truly made this book possible. They have shared their stories and insights generously. We deeply appreciate the enthusiasm and positive inspiration of all of the folks we have been privileged to interact with.

Finally, we would like to thank Phyllis (aka "Mom"), who has always been supportive of our endeavors. Brett, thanks for asking us "how's that book coming along?" every time you called! It was incentive to have to report our progress every week. We appreciate the support and feedback.

❶

AN INTRODUCTION

"There are so many positive things about my identity."

This book starts a new conversation with inspiring narratives that reveal and embrace positive lesbian, gay, bisexual, transgender, and queer (LGBTQ) identities. In this book, we present eight life-affirming themes for cultivating positive LGBTQ identities.[1] These themes show clearly how LGBTQ identities can be an important part of thriving and flourishing lives.

Consider the following stories.

Catherine, a 21-year-old college student, comes to her family home in the Northeast on a Saturday afternoon to have lunch with her mother. She's a little nervous, so before her mother even finishes making their sandwiches, she blurts out, "Mom, I want to tell you that I'm a lesbian. I really want to be honest with you because I feel like that's the next step in my being able to grow as a person. I've already learned a lot about myself in thinking about this and in figuring out how I feel and what I want in life." Catherine feels relief at being honest with her mother. Her mother looks up from the sandwiches, gives her daughter a hug, and says, "Honey, that's great! I appreciate that you are being honest with me. I think it'll bring us closer together. I'd love it if you would share with me the things you've been thinking about. Now, before we sit down to talk, do you want some mayo on your sandwich?"

On the other side of the country, 30-something M.J. sits down with two coworkers (John and David) for lunch. They talk about their upcoming weekend plans. M.J. reveals plans to go to a "Trans Pride March" on Saturday. David says, "That's cool. What's this march about?" M.J. replies, "It's about many things. We're trying to get unisex restrooms in different public places in the city so that trans people can feel safe, and it's great for families with small kids too. And we are pushing for marriage equality so that any couple can get married. And we want to push more companies to have inclusive nondiscrimination policies and provide inclusive health care for trans people." John interrupts with a question: "Are you all going to protest the new immigration restrictions? That has to affect transgender people too." M.J. answers, "I was at a rally last weekend protesting those bills. I'm sure a lot of people in the community will be there with signs and petitions. Everyone needs to be treated with respect." M.J.'s friends look at each other, smile, and say, "This rocks! Can we come too?"

We hope these positive interactions make you smile. And, yes, there are people out there who just said, "Hey, that's exactly what happened to me!" But, be honest, a few of you just rolled your eyes. For many of us who identify as lesbian, gay, bisexual, transgender, or queer (or any of the many variations of these identities), we read these stories and smile, thinking "I wish that was my experience." We, the authors, want to help make it more likely that people with LGBTQ identities have positive feelings about themselves and experience positive interactions with others. We want everyone to recognize the positive aspects of LGBTQ identities. We want to start a new conversation by fully embracing the positive narratives about LGBTQ lives.

While we have heard many positive stories with happy endings, we admit that we also hear stories that go something like this: "I went home and told my mother that I'm gay. The only thing she said was that maybe my brother would give her grandchildren and that she knew I would be miserable for the rest of my life." Or the story of a young woman telling her friends that she's bisexual. Her friends replied, "That's too bad. You're so pretty and you could be so happy. Maybe you'll find a man and settle down and forget all this nonsense." What you will see as you read this book is that even this type of less-than-positive encounter can serve to make LGBTQ people more aware of their personal strengths as they form positive identities. Ultimately we want LGBTQ identities to be celebrated. The more positive stories we see, hear, and read about, the more such narratives become reality for everyone.

All people, including LGBTQ people, need to develop a positive identity in order to flourish. The society that we live in is not always supportive of LGBTQ identities, so we need a strong sense of self to counter any negative messages we experience. Many of the people who tell us that we won't be happy, or far more negative things, are reflecting the negative things they've heard about lesbian, gay, bisexual, transgender, and queer people. Some of these people are well-meaning and honestly concerned for us—just *very misguided* in their attempts at what they call "support." What they need are new, more positive ways of supporting us. They need to hear the truth—that LGBTQ people are leading lives filled with meaning, purpose, and happiness. LGBTQ people themselves need to hear stories that support their positive identity and strength development.

Negative stories about LGBTQ identities have negative consequences for the well-being of LGBTQ people (and their families and friends), especially if there is a lack of positive stories to counter the negative. For example, Michael, a middle-aged gay man, told us that when he was first coming out he wasn't happy because he had heard that being gay meant he would never have a loving, committed relationship. He believed that negative stereotype, common in his culture. Michael did not have any positive stories or role models to support his identity and correct the misinformation he received. However, we know from research studies that this negative stereotype is not based in reality. The majority of gay men are in loving, committed relationships (and now so is Michael).[2] So while we may hear a lot of negative messages, we know that the reality is far more positive. Let's talk about those positive stories!

In fact, there are many positive things about gay, lesbian, bisexual, transgender, and queer identities. The truth is that most LGBTQ people are leading happy and fulfilling lives. We just don't hear those stories as often or see them portrayed in the media very much. That omission is an oversight that we believe is important to address. We'll say it again—there are many positive aspects to having lesbian, gay, bisexual, transgender, and queer identities! In our empirically based research, we discovered eight positive themes common to LGBTQ identities. Those themes are

- living an authentic life;
- having increased self-awareness and insight;
- feeling free to create flexible rules for what gender means and how it is expressed;
- experiencing strong emotional connections with others and creating supportive families of choice;
- exploring expressions of sexuality and creating intimate relationships with "new rules";
- having a unique perspective on life with empathy and compassion for others;
- being a positive role model, mentor, and activist working for social justice;
- belonging to an LGBTQ community.

These eight themes are key answers to the question, "What is positive about having a lesbian, gay, bisexual, transgender, or queer identity?" We have asked this question of more than one thousand LGBTQ-identified people, and this book summarizes their answers. At their roots, these themes are positive feelings and actions that apply to all adults, whether younger or older, whether male, female, or transgender, and regardless of whether an individual is just coming out or has been out for decades.

This book is for people who came out a long time ago and are looking for ideas about how to flourish in their lives. This book is for people who are just coming out and want to read positive narratives and find positive meaning in their experiences and identities. Whether you come out at 16 or 61 (or 91!), we hope that this book will help you reflect on the positive aspects of a diverse array of sexual and gender identities. Let's face it: most of us are just plain interested in hearing other LGBTQ peoples' experiences of their identities and find it affirming to hear these positive stories.[3]

These positive stories include our relationship with ourselves, our relationships with others, and our interactions with the broader community. Most telling, the themes represent positive stories of strength and insights into the psychological benefits of LGBTQ identities.[4] Yes, we said benefits!

This book is also for people who are not completely out or not out to anyone but themselves. In fact, some of the people we interviewed had not disclosed their identities to very many others. There are many ways to grow and flourish regardless of how out we are or how much we disclose about our identities to others. Positive stories support us in the process of coming out to ourselves, coming out to others, and just living our lives.

The themes in this book reflect core values about self and relationships that are accessible to everyone. For example, everyone can reflect on how their identity, especially one that they might choose not to disclose, can bring about feelings of empathy for others. We may enjoy a sense of community online with people in other locations. We can be positive role models for others and work for social justice in a variety of ways. For adolescents and young adults, reading about the positive aspects of LGBTQ identities may be a step toward coming out or having a better understanding of their feelings. For some, having positive stories or a positive perspective may simply be a source of private relief and support.

This book is also for allies, family members, friends, business and human resources professionals, and service providers for the LGBTQ community. Service providers include psychologists, social workers, mental health professionals, doctors, nurses, medical staff, lawyers, pastors, teachers, and school counselors. This book is for anyone who works with LGBTQ-identified or questioning individuals and their families.

This is a book about development and growth. The things we talk about in this book are ways to improve the quality of people's lives. Anyone interested in reflecting on what makes a life positive and fulfilling, regardless of their sexual or gender identity, may want to read this book.[5] Of course, you do not have to do or experience all of the things in this book to feel happy or fulfilled. In fact, not one of the participants in our research mentioned all eight themes. We (the authors) did not list all eight when we gave our answers! Leading a fulfilling life is about the quality of the activities we engage in and the meaning we find in these activities.

We suggest that you read through the themes and exercises in each chapter, finding those that appeal most to you. Try engaging in even one activity related to any one of these themes. See how it feels for you.[6] Does it make a positive difference in your outlook on life? You may discover ways to create more positive narratives in your life. You may feel more fulfilled. Reading this book can help you to reflect on how to engage in positive, identity-enhancing actions. It may also be helpful to share your positive stories with your loved ones. It is important for those who care about you to hear these positive stories and realize the many positive aspects of LGBTQ identities.

ASKING AN IMPORTANT QUESTION

The idea for this book started back in 2004, a few weeks after the November election. One of the authors (Ellen) was taking a walk with our friend and neighbor (Sue). Members of the LGBTQ community in Kentucky were very disappointed, sad, and angry (to name just a few of the negative emotions we heard about) after voters passed a marriage restriction amendment to the state constitution. Our talk turned to the negative impact that the public debate and passage of the amendment had on the health and well-being of the community. Negative messages about gays and lesbians were seemingly all around, and discrimination against same-sex relationships had just been voted into the state constitution by a large margin. Sue was aggravated by all of this and asked, "What are the good things about being a lesbian? I want to hear about the positive things." The same question of course applies to people who identify as gay, bisexual, transgender, and queer. Simply put, it's a great question!

Being good scholars, when faced with a timely and intriguing question, we conduct research! So we posted an online survey where we asked lesbian, gay, bisexual, transgender, and queer-identified individuals to tell us what they thought were the positive things about their LGBTQ identities. Our survey seemed to strike a chord with the community. We received a lot of answers to our surveys in a short period of time. Almost a thousand people from all over the United States and a few other countries (mostly Canada and Great Britain, but also Australia and New Zealand) responded. We published three academic journal articles summarizing the results. We invite you to read these original articles.[7]

We received a lot of e-mails from people thanking us for asking the question! For example, one person wrote, "Writing this has reminded me of how positive it is to be a bisexually identified person. Thank you for the opportunity!" Another person reflected in an e-mail, "No one has ever asked me this question before. I thought I wouldn't be able to think of anything, but once I started, I was amazed at how much positive there is. Thank you. I'm going ask my friends this question and see what they say."

Sometimes just asking the right question is a form of "therapy."[8] The right question can direct people to reframe or think in a different way about themselves or others. How many times are LGBTQ folks asked about the positive aspects of their lives? Judging from the feedback we received, not often enough—if ever. We think that needs to change for the better. We need to think about and talk about the positive aspects of our lives!

Some of the people who took our online surveys e-mailed us to ask for the results of the study. They were curious about what other people had to say. This book represents an expanded response to those requests. LGBTQ individuals who are working to create positive meaning, well-being, and health in their lives can use this information to reflect on their experiences and recognize opportunities for continued personal growth and development.

MULTIPLE IDENTITIES AND LABELS

We asked specifically about lesbian, gay, bisexual, and transgender identities in our surveys and interviews. A significant number of people in these surveys also self-identified as "queer." We did not define any of these terms for our research participants. Instead, we allowed them to decide for themselves whether any of these labels were a part of their identity. Therefore, *lesbian* may include additional labels such as "woman-loving-woman" and "dyke." Likewise, some gay men may prefer the designation of "man-loving-man." Men, women, and transgender individuals may identify themselves as *gay* and/or *queer*. Bisexual identity may include persons in heterosexual relationships as well as those in same-sex relationships or in relationships that they do not identify as either heterosexual or same-sex.

"Lesbian," "gay," and "bisexual" are labels that refer to *sexual* identities. Transgender, on the other hand, includes a wide spectrum of identities and labels referring to *gender* identity. Transgender includes those who do not identify with or conform to the gender or the sex they are assigned at birth. Transgender may include "genderqueers," that is, those who identify as *neither* male nor female, or *both* male and female, and express their gender in ways that are considered *neither* feminine nor masculine, or *both* feminine and masculine. People who identify as transsexual or intersex may also identify with the term *transgender*. Some transgender people specifically identify as "MTF" (male-to-female) or "FTM" (female-to-male) to indicate a sex or gender transition. Gay men, lesbians, and bisexual-identified individuals may identify as transgender and/or queer as part of their sexual and gender identity.

"Queer" may be the broadest identity label we include. The term *queer* has traditionally been used to describe something out of the ordinary or unconventional. There is no simple definition of queer as an identity. Queer may refer to either sexual or gender identity, or a combination of the two. Queer may include people who reject the norms of "straight" identity or who have a sexual or gender identity that does not meet conventional expectations.[9] In the context of this book, because we did not direct our surveys to a "queer community" or ask specifically about "queer identity," we use this term broadly. In our descriptions of individuals we are quoting, we use "queer" as a label *when* and *how* that individual chooses to use it.

Some people, on the other hand, do not identify with any of these labels or told us specifically, *"I don't like labels"* (see chapter 4 for more on this). We support every person's right to self-identify, with or without labels.[10] People might prefer one of many different labels.[11] Or to use more than one label. These labels may not mean the same thing to everyone. In our research, we try to provide opportunities for individuals to describe themselves, and we often use those self-descriptions in this book.[12] So when the reader sees, for example, "gay, queer, transgender" (in quotation marks) as a description for someone we are quoting, that means we are directly quoting the multiple labels with which that person identifies.

Some members of racial or ethnic minority groups do not identify with the labels of lesbian, gay, bisexual, transgender, or queer. These labels may be seen as applying mostly to the white/Caucasian community. A 33-year-old Latina woman from Toronto, Canada, makes this point clear: "It is hard to label my own understandings of my desires. I think that in the Queer of Colour Community in which I locate myself, we have other ways of understanding the diverse sexualities available to us. We don't use the same labels as the White Community because they don't mean the same thing to us."

In an attempt to be more inclusive of those in communities that use different words or have different meanings for LGBTQ, we included some alternative descriptions in our survey announcements, such as "man-loving-man," "woman-loving-woman," or "same-gender-loving." We realize that even these broad terms do not always capture the multitude of ways that people think of or describe themselves and that some people may not have felt included even though we were trying to be as inclusive as possible. However, as you read you will see evidence of the creative variety of labels, and combinations of labels, that people use to describe their complex sexual and gender identities.

To complicate things even further, LGBTQ people have multiple identities in addition to their sexual identities and gender identities. That is, they identify as LGBTQ and also, for example, as a person of color, or as a hearing-impaired person, or as Jewish or Catholic.[13] One young man we spoke with explained his multiple identities: "I'm a 'black gay' man. The reason I say that in that order is because I guess in a sense I knew I was black long before I knew I was gay. But I think the two have been very helpful to one another in how I understand both identities." This young man likely could have added other identities as well. LGBTQ people have other circumstances that impact their lives and identities, such as living in a rural area, or working in a factory, or being a student. Simply put, each LGBTQ person is unique. However, because of similarities of experience, the positive aspects of LGBTQ identities we discuss in this book seem to have wide applicability.

Our experience is that even individuals who do not want to be labeled themselves or who use creative self-labels are often looking for role models who identify as lesbian, gay, bisexual, transgender, or queer. Therefore, we hope this book can be inspiring regardless of the self-identity of the reader. In fact, we hope it is inspiring to straight people as well as members of the LGBTQ and sexual minority communities. Read on and see what resonates with your experience and identities.

MINORITY STRESS, COPING, AND RESILIENCE

Since 2001, we have conducted several studies of the health and well-being of LGBTQ individuals and same-sex couples. For example, we have interviewed more than one hundred same-sex couples about the meaning of commitment in their long-term relationships and how they cope with the challenges of being a same-sex couple.[14] We have also gathered stories about same-sex couples' experiences with their families and at work,[15] how they deal with relationship status issues (including marriage and legal issues),[16] and their relationship to religious or spiritual communities.[17] We have surveyed thousands of LGBTQ individuals about these topics and about other stresses and challenges in their lives, including the marriage restriction amendments and the debates surrounding those public campaigns.[18]

Much of our research explores the ways LGBTQ people are impacted by "minority stress." Minority stress is a chronic or long-term social stress, over and above the general stressors of daily life. It is additional stress solely related, in this case, to LGBTQ identities. Minority stress leads to the negative effects on health and well-being that are caused by social stigmatization.[19]

For LGBTQ individuals, minority stress includes actual experiences of discrimination as well as the anticipation of rejection because of our LGBTQ identities. Minority stress includes the stress of hiding and concealing our identity from others. LGBTQ people may experience internalized homonegativity (sometimes called internalized homophobia) because they are subjected to and believe negative narratives and stereotypes about LGBTQ identities. Minority stress also includes the coping strategies that LGBT individuals develop to deal with all of these other stresses.[20] These coping strategies, some positive and some not-so-positive, require energy to enact. In short, minority stress has been linked with some serious issues that negatively impact the health and well-being of LGBTQ individuals, their families, and the community.[21]

One of the lessons we quickly learned was that studying minority stress is, well, stressful! As researchers we try to remain as objective as possible. But as human beings and members of the LGBTQ community, we are touched and even changed by the stories of those who participate in our studies. We are fortunate to have had the opportunity to hear the stories of thousands of LGBTQ people and their families over the past decade. We feel it is part of our responsibility to share our discoveries in support of positive changes. We feel that passing along positive stories will counteract and, hopefully, relieve some minority stress. In this way we hope to contribute to enhancing the conditions where LGBTQ people can flourish.

SOCIAL CONTEXT OF MINORITY STRESS

"It's not magic like they make it look like on TV. It's hard work to come out, and everything doesn't always go right. On TV it's like everything's okay by the end of the show, but in real life that doesn't happen. It's not magically okay by the end of the day." That's what one gay teenager told us about his experience of coming out. Even though the tone of this book is positive, we do not minimize, deny, or dismiss the real suffering, anxiety, and distress that LGBTQ people can feel. However, it is essential and healthy to also recognize that stories of distress are not the only stories out there. There are positive stories and positive outlooks. These positive stories can help us see our lives in new, more positive ways.

Several current contextual factors exacerbate minority stress. One of the most pressing issues contributing to minority stress is bullying of LGBTQ adolescents and young adults in schools. Bullying also takes place in workplaces and other social places, such as online social networks. People who are perceived as LGBTQ or an ally of LGBTQ people are at risk for being targets of bullying. Bullying is epidemic; it has a negative impact by socially excluding, intimidating, or threatening people and may include acts of physical aggression and violence.[22]

It is extremely important to counteract the negative and destructive effects of bullying. First, persons who are bullied should feel empowered to act in positive ways to report and stop the bullying.[23] Second, teachers, counselors, supervisors, and any person in a position of authority should feel empowered to act in positive and decisive ways to stop bullying. However, we know from research studies that many people do not feel competent to deal effectively with bullying, especially anti-LGBTQ bullying.[24] Some teachers and leaders have only heard negative narratives about LGBTQ people and have not received training in positive approaches to affirming LGBTQ identities. This book can help fill that void in training by providing positive reference points.

State or institutional prejudice, such as the lack of marriage equality or not being included in nondiscrimination laws or policies, exacerbates minority stress.[25] These policies (or lack of policies) support negative stereotypes and beliefs about LGBTQ identities. The political debates surrounding these issues are often filled with negative stereotypes and hateful anti-LGBTQ rhetoric. Positive stories help to correct these misrepresentations. Positive stories are also an important tool of empowerment for the community. By sharing narratives of strength and empowerment we can inspire each other to take positive action against discriminatory policies.

A final contextual source of minority stress that we will mention here (although there are many more) is religious intolerance. There are many open and affirming religious institutions. These supportive religious institutions stand in contrast to religious institutions that deny recognition to the spiritual humanity of LGBTQ people. Many LGBTQ people struggle with negative messages they were taught in their religious communities. Intolerant religious institutions use their public position of authority to work against LGBTQ equality and acceptance. Sharing stories of our common humanity, spiritual values, and commitments may help everyone to see that true compassion, acceptance of difference, and inclusion are necessary for all people to lead fulfilling lives with meaning and purpose, including spiritual meanings.

A MEANINGFUL LIFE

As we gathered stories from LGBTQ participants for our research, we were struck by the strength, courage, and optimism of the individuals and couples that we met. While our participants did, indeed, experience minority stress in their lives, this was far from the whole story. In the stories about the challenges they encounter, we also find the stories of their strengths. We find people who are living happy and satisfying lives. These people see many more positives than negatives about their lives and relationships. Everyone tries to make sense of the world around them and make meaning in their lives.[26] LGBTQ people clearly use their identities as opportunity to create positive meaning.

It is important that we look at our lives and ask what small action we might take to make things just a little bit better. We need to look at what has special meaning for us and ask how we can expand that meaning in our lives. Practicing or reflecting on the themes in this book may help you to feel happier, more satisfied, or more fulfilled. However, this book is not meant to be a surefire prescription for happiness. It is a guide to exploring what works for you. If some of these affirmations seem out of reach at any given time, just keep exploring. Our lives are always a work in progress.

Human beings are storytellers. The stories we tell ourselves and others help to shape our thoughts, feelings, and actions. It is important that we pay attention to our own stories and look for our positive strengths when facing challenges in our lives. A 42-year-old gay man living in Connecticut finds this to be true: "I find great delight in being a gay man. I think I'm more open-minded than my straight friends. Of course, I don't wish to turn this into a gay vs. straight competition, but sometimes it seems that way. I think because we've been kicked in the teeth a few too many times, we're a very resilient group. We know how to change a negative into a positive."[27]

A few people who responded to our surveys told us that they perceived nothing positive about their LGBTQ identities. A few told us that their sexual or gender identities are neither positive nor negative, "*it just is*" or it is "*just who I am.*" Some of these folks did not add anything else. Others went on to tell us several positive things, because once they started thinking about the question and reflecting on their lives, they did have a positive view of their LGBTQ identity and what it contributed to their lives. Indeed, it is as Frank Kameny said in 1968, "*Gay is Good*"—and we would add, "*Lesbian, Bisexual, Transgender, and Queer are Good*" too.[28]

Two noted psychologists wrote that for persons of color, pride in one's race and ethnicity and the experiences of oppression "sharpen and hone [one's] survival skills to such a degree that these skills are now deemed to be assets."[29] We suggest that the same process may well apply to LGBTQ persons—in facing adversity, we may transform our experiences into personal growth. As such, this book is about cultivating a positive self, one that benefits ourselves as well as those around us.

OVERVIEW OF THE BOOK

The themes presented in the following chapters reflect values of compassion and generosity extended to the self as well as to others. Each theme has implications for the self, the self in relation to others, and the self within a larger community of people. These levels of interaction are interdependent; as we make changes in one part of our lives, these changes impact the other parts of our lives.

The reader will notice overlap between the themes presented in the chapters that follow. For instance, as we become more authentic in our self-expression, we strengthen our connections to others. As we strengthen our connections to others, we feel more empathy and compassion for communities of people we connect with. As we feel more compassion for these communities, we may find ourselves working in support of social justice. This work, as an expression of our values, in turn strengthens our sense of authenticity. The numerous interconnections will become even clearer as you read the chapters.

In each chapter we discuss one of the eight positive themes for LGBTQ identities based on our empirical study and analysis. We illustrate each theme with stories from people we have interviewed online or in person. We include stories from additional sources also. In most cases we quote the words that people use to describe the essence of their identity.[30] Of course, we change some of the details of stories and descriptions to protect participants' confidentiality or to make stories shorter and easier to read.

In each chapter, we present brief summaries of what we know (as scholars and practitioners) about why each theme is a positive aspect of identity. We draw most often on recent research from positive, social, and critical psychology and strength-based counseling to support the importance of each theme to individual lives.

We end each chapter with some questions to reflect on or exercises to try. These activities are intended to help you to explore each theme and its applications to your life. We offer suggestions for reflecting on each theme and for trying out new behaviors to support and strengthen the positive aspects of LGBTQ identities. We hope that by reading this book and trying some of the exercises, you will have an opportunity to explore, more systematically than you might otherwise, positive emotions and experiences in life. By thinking about the positives more systematically, hopefully you will find more enjoyment in life. More ways to connect to others. More meaning, joy, and happiness.

Finally, we end the book with some additional resources. These websites are not a comprehensive list by any stretch of the imagination. The list of resources available is growing all the time. A quick search on the web will help you find updates and new resources.

As you finish reading this introduction, take a few moments to think about what you find to be positive about your lesbian, gay, bisexual, transgender, or queer identities (or straight, or choose any word that you feel best describes you today). Then read the rest of the book and see what resonates with your experience. Don't be surprised if you find yourself thinking, "I could have written that!" Or perhaps you will find yourself, for example, as a gay man, agreeing with a bisexual woman or a "trans-straight man." You may find a new understanding of LGBTQ identities and a new appreciation for your own life experiences. Read on to find out more.

②

AUTHENTICITY

"I can be myself and be more authentic with others."

"Just be yourself!" How many times have we heard these words or something like them? These words are typically meant to encourage us. They are often said to reassure us that we are wonderful people, and if we will just "be ourselves," then other people will get to know us and see our good qualities. Get to know us and appreciate us. Fall in love with us. Trust us. Or any number of other good outcomes.

Of course, hearing these words, "just be yourself," can also bring on an existential crisis—"Who am I?!" Many of us have serious questions about how to just be ourselves. And many of us have multiple selves: one identity at school or work, a different identity at home, and maybe yet another identity when we are out with friends. Being ourselves means getting to the core of our own values and beliefs so that we can express ourselves fully and honestly.[1] This is the essence of what we mean by *authenticity*.

If a part of our identity is lesbian, gay, bisexual, transgender, queer, or any combination of these (and other identities), then living our life authentically is an exciting and interesting journey. Hundreds of autobiographies and biographies, books, movies, and websites tell the stories of LGBTQ people who have gone through the process of creating an authentic life.[2] There are many challenges in this process. There are also many rewards.

Living authentically means figuring out who we are, speaking as truthfully as we are able, and being as genuine as we can with others.[3] It doesn't mean always being totally out or disclosing everything about ourselves to every single person we meet. It does mean being honest with ourselves and using the strengths we find within to be the best we can be in this world.

In the stories we have gathered, some people explain that being authentic means simply "being who I am" or "it's just who I am." Others tell us, with a sense of relief, that living authentically means that "I don't have to hide who I am" or "I don't have to live my life as a lie." These simple yet profound statements of authenticity portray the satisfaction that comes from discovering who we are and then embodying and expressing that discovery in everyday life.[4] In general, the more authentic we are, the more hopeful we are, the less depressed we are, and the more positive feelings we have about life.[5] Authenticity is an important contributor to our well-being.

In our studies, the journey to authenticity is overall the most frequently mentioned positive aspect of LGBTQ identities. This journey includes the lessons learned from our life experiences, the feeling of being "true to myself," and being able to "just be me." For example, a 40-year-old lesbian from Colorado explains how *honesty* is an integral part of her authentic expression of her identity:

> The single most positive aspect of being a lesbian is honesty. I'm honest about who I am, and that honesty creates a lot of comfort in my life because I find I'm happiest when I act and live my life as honestly as possible. When I am honest I feel there is less chance to be hurt emotionally. Besides, being honest about who I am eliminates the nagging question of 'Would you still love me if you knew?'

An integral part of the coming-out or transition experience is authenticity.[6] The lessons learned about authenticity will likely influence other parts of our lives and can lead to the development of other character strengths such as wisdom, vitality, spirituality, and courage.[7] A 36-year-old Native American "FTM straight man" living in New Mexico made a particularly apt observation about learning some major life lessons:

"Transition taught me courage, truthfulness, authenticity, love, acceptance, honor—all of the things pop psychology books try to sell." We're glad you are reading this book, but in the end, we know it is the lessons from your own life that will help you to flourish. We want to help you recognize some of those lessons.

DISCOVERING OUR AUTHENTIC SELF

The coming-out process starts with being in touch with ourselves about our identity and feelings (we also talk about this in chapter 3). Most of us who identify as LGBTQ have to discover, acknowledge, and affirm this part of ourselves *actively*.[8] Becoming aware of our romantic attractions, our sexuality, and our gender identity can be a long process, requiring great effort and courage for some. For some, it may be a shorter process. And for others it may not seem like much of a process at all.

Hearing ourselves claim our identity out loud can help us in our process of self-acceptance. To say that we have a lesbian, gay, bisexual, transgender, or queer identity can be a very powerful step in acknowledging our true self and living authentically. Having someone else hear us or recognize our authentic self is affirming.

Coming out by actively acknowledging to ourselves and others our sexual and/or gender identity is usually necessary because, unless we tell them otherwise, others typically assume that we are heterosexual or the sex listed on our birth certificate. Questioning the assumption that we are heterosexual and allowing ourselves to consider our same-sex attractions can be important acts that lead to self-discovery. Questioning the sex (male or female) recorded on our birth certificate can be a step toward exploring our true identity. Asking these questions of ourselves about our experiences often leads to deeper levels of self-awareness and insight, which we also discuss in chapter 3.

Discovering and expressing our sexual and gender identities optimally leads to self-acceptance and authentic living. The positive emotions that accompany self-acceptance give us the energy and vitality that we need to interact positively in our relationships, at work, and in our communities. For example, identifying as bisexual may allow some people to validate the range of their experiences of attraction and sexual expression and thus achieve a more complete sense of their authentic selves. For a 36-year-old "bisexual, queer female" this is a key point: "It's an honest description of who I am, despite pressure on me from gays and straights to 'pick' one of their sexual orientations instead. To proudly identify as bisexual for seventeen years is to affirm every romantic and sexual relationship I've had as valid and not apologize for past relationships or a key part of my life to appease my peers."

Claiming LGBTQ identities may lead to a sense of *"wholeness."* Several people describe their experience as being "more at home with myself." A 25-year-old "lesbian-identified queer bisexual" residing in New Hampshire describes herself as a blossoming flower, a delightfully positive metaphor for the journey of self-discovery and acceptance:

> Rather than being 'this not that,' I'm 'this AND that.' I've felt like a blossoming flower. As I become more fully me and as I'm more comfortable with each petal of my identity, I open myself up and look into the sun . . . as someone who identifies as bisexual and does see the world on a multitude of planes, my intellect and creativity, my head and my heart, are just further parallels of how I am able to find myself attracted to and love both men and women.

When we "blossom," we may want to share that news with others. When we share our authentic self with others, we hope to experience acceptance. At times this feels risky, because we don't know how others will respond or how we will feel once we disclose our identity. Feeling anxious is a normal reaction to taking a risk. Finding the courage and determination to take the risk, even in the face of anxiety, is a key to living authentically. When we claim our identity out loud, it often becomes more *real* to us as well as to others.

The literature in psychology includes several classic models of the coming-out process. These models describe several steps in the process and often begin with being honest with oneself about sexual attractions and gender identity. Later steps involve disclosing that identity to others and acting authentically in the world.[9]

Being truthful with ourselves is a sign of positive self-regard. It is a sign that we can be self-aware and that we value our self (see chapter 3). When we are truthful or authentic with another person, we express our belief in our own intrinsic worth. A 64-year-old "man-loving-man" from

Texas expresses the importance of honesty: "What counts is how you treat yourself with honesty, self-love, and the ability to be openly honest with your partner and others. That's the important part of owning my identity." Authenticity in our relationships can enhance closeness in our relationships (see chapter 5).[10] Finding others who support and encourage the expression of our authentic self is important to our well-being. Acknowledging and expressing ourselves authentically, especially to others who will support our expression of our authentic self, are the courageous acts that blaze our trail on the journey to "just be yourself."

LIVING AN AUTHENTIC LIFE

Claiming our LGBT identities is an act of self-empowerment and may enhance our sense of well-being.[11] Living our life authentically, even though it may feel risky at times, facilitates personal growth. Coming to love and appreciate ourselves for who we are frees up our energy to pursue goals and activities that are meaningful to us.

Self-acceptance and authentic expression are accompanied by personal growth, which we also talk about in chapter 3. A 57-year-old "trans-woman" from Arizona makes this observation about how authentic self-expression led to her personal growth:

> The transition in crossing genders was a spiritual adventure for me. Facing all the fears that are there, such as losing one's job, losing friends, losing finances and one's home was very fearful. Facing those fears, and realizing that I was willing to lose all those things to be myself, was a sacred and spiritual experience. To walk thru the possibilities of losing everything gave me an understanding of what the Buddhists call 'attachments to desires,' and when I lost those attachments, it felt as though I had entered a new world, where everything is possible, and magic is all around.

Growing in self-acceptance of our sexual and gender identities often accompanies growth in other parts of our lives. To live authentically includes "following our bliss" by pursuing activities that we are passionate about. Being who we are might mean expressing ourselves as, say, an artist, an accountant, an athlete, a salesperson, a farmer, or a teacher. "Striving mightily for goals that [we] value"[12] increases our sense of well-being, even though the pursuit may be filled with ups and downs, successes and failures. Engaging fully with life, bringing our authentic self to our pursuits and passions, is part of a life well lived.

Successfully meeting the challenges of embracing and celebrating our gender and sexual identities can free us to grow and develop other aspects of ourselves. A gay man, 39, from Washington State sees the interconnections and embraces all parts of his identity: "Being a gay man has made me realize that I can be myself, that I can do the work I want to do [being artistic and creative] without fear of being called gay—because I am and I own that right along with my artistic abilities." Devoting our energy to fully developing our unique talents and abilities and working to achieve personally meaningful goals that contribute to our community is part of what is called *self-actualization*.[13]

Living authentically may also be expressed in a positive and far-reaching enthusiasm for life. For example, a 43-year-old lesbian living in Missouri explains the broad impact on her life of living authentically: "I am living authentically, which feeds my confidence, my joy and happiness, my relationship with God, my improved health." Another lesbian, a 42-year-old woman living in Arkansas who had recently come out, also experiences a range of benefits: "I think knowing who you really are and embracing yourself is very important and positive. It allows you to reach your full potential and to be authentic. It has helped me in many other areas of my life as well, in my relationships with friends, and at work."

Achieving an integrated life often means moving from a life that feels fragmented or compartmentalized into a sense that each of us is the same person across all of our relationships and roles, inside our bodies and in our outward expressions. This kind of integration or authenticity across all parts of our lives can be a long and challenging process of personal growth and development that requires patience, perseverance, good role models, and the emotional support of friends. For some people this process starts early in life; for others it begins later. For all, this process is ongoing.

People with LGBTQ identities are not the only ones who have to deal with questions of authenticity and integrity. Allies of the LGBTQ community have their own processes of discovering and claiming an identity.

Allies also need to figure out how to live authentically and truthfully within themselves and with others.[14]

OUR AUTHENTIC STYLE

As we discover who we are and celebrate that discovery, we often come up with ways to express ourselves that are congruent with this self-knowledge and self-acceptance. We may express our authentic self through our style and manner of dress. If we think about it, this makes sense. No one can see what is going on inside of us, so our most visible outward action is our appearance.

Some LGBTQ people talk about style, fashion, and just *being comfortable* in their clothes as a way to express who they are. The way we dress can be an expression that makes our identity more visible to others. Or it may just be a way to make a statement to ourselves, making us feel good about ourselves. To express ourselves authentically in a visible way may increase our self-confidence or raise our self-esteem.

Every person has an individual style. Many LGBTQ people have talked to us about how their style is an important statement and a positive part of their identity. Within any of these identities, LGBTQ, a wide range of styles is expressed by individuals. Some styles may be consistent with a stereotype. Yes, some lesbians do wear flannel shirts! Others are not consistent with cultural stereotypes, such as the big, football-playing tough guy in stained, sweaty gray clothes (who also happens to be gay). So even though we make some generalizations below, we are not claiming that this is the full extent of stylishness in the LGBTQ community.

For some gay men, having fashion sense and dressing in a particular way is a part of showing that they are, well, "fabulous!" Some might cringe and say that the exceedingly well-dressed gay man is just a stereotype. Others embrace and celebrate their style sense and find a freedom in expressing their identity through their clothes. For example, on the one hand, a 34-year-old gay man from Florida embraces what some might think of as a stereotype as part of his style: "I like being able to dress well and wear colors and things that straight men might not wear. I like wearing pink shirts because I do look pretty in pink!" On the other hand, a 50-year-old gay man from New York notes that wearing pink would not be an authentic expression of his identity. He has his own style: "I dress very masculine. Just because I'm gay doesn't mean that I am not masculine. I think it screws with some people's stereotypes that I don't wear pink and that I wear nice suits and ties and probably look straight. In that way, just being me challenges people's stereotypes and makes them broaden their views."

For some lesbians, style or manner of dress is about comfort and being themselves instead of trying to "conform to the cultural ideal of the feminine woman." Self-expression may include embracing their strength and reflecting that in their clothes. As a 35-year-old gay woman from Minnesota notes, "I can be athletic and strong wherever I am without trying to be feminine or ladylike to make up for it. I can wear big black work boots or running shoes. I don't have to wear heels and dresses to convince someone that I'm feminine. This is my idea of feminine." From boots to heels, flannel shirts to dresses, lesbians take advantage of a range of style and choices. For example, a 27-year-old lesbian from California enjoys the wide range of expression available to her: "I can express all sides of myself when I get dressed—I can wear a men's suit today, a dress tomorrow. I don't have to worry about dressing to attract a man like my straight friends. I just have to dress as myself."

For some people who identify as transgender or genderqueer, authenticity can include congruency between their inner feelings and outer appearances. A 32-year-old "transman" living in Maryland refers to Mark Twain's famous saying, "Clothes make the man," to explain the importance of "dressing as my true self so that others can see me the way that I do." The way a person dresses is a form of self-expression that makes a visual statement to others. For a transgender 18-year-old from Ohio who had just graduated from high school, that's the point of clothes: "I can wear any clothes I like since neither men's nor women's clothing really applies (or fits properly). I like to dress gender-ambiguous to keep people guessing. That way I make transgender people more visible."

While some of us may look at picking out clothes and getting dressed as a necessary chore, for a 56-year-old "normal woman" from Mississippi, the act of getting dressed and ready for the day is a freeing expression of her authentic self: "I love the time-consuming, change-my-mind routine of picking out the clothes I will wear each day; washing, brushing, and drying my hair just right; getting the makeup just right for the demands or fun of each day; and matching the right jewelry to each outfit and occasion. It was so dreary and dreadful having to wear male clothes, and I feel free of all that at last."

CONGRUENT IDENTITY

Claiming a transgender or genderqueer identity allowed several people we interviewed to express an "honesty," "truth," and "unity within myself" that they had not previously experienced. Before transitioning, some transgender individuals felt that they had been living with a "sense of denial toward a true part of my personhood." Expressing their authentic sex or gender brought about feelings of "true peace," "relief," and "being whole." These feelings may apply to people who identify as lesbian, gay, bisexual, or queer as well. However, the process of transition or gender-congruent expression may hold special importance as part of a positive identity for transgender or genderqueer individuals.[15]

A psychological transition may accompany the physical transition. A 37-year-old "straight man" from Texas transitioned from a female body to a male body and experienced "an exterior that I and others can more readily identify with. I can live the life that I know should be mine. This identity has brought me happiness, a feeling of wholeness, well-being, truth, unity. It truly is about being whole, happy, and peaceful." These feelings are part of a change that can be transformational in many positive ways.

Congruency of inner and outer body is, for some, like finding the missing piece of a puzzle so that they feel complete. For some, this congruence includes stopping the forced façade of their assigned sex and instead living as their true self. As a 63-year-old woman who "lived in a male shell most of my life" explains, "Expressing my female identity as the real me to people has had a calming effect on me and has allowed me to begin growing as a complete person for the first time in my life."

A CAUTION

We feel that it is important to acknowledge that some types of self-expression can be risky at certain times or in some locations. When

LGBTQ people hear "just be yourself," it may not always sound friendly or encouraging at all. It may sound like a recipe for rejection. (By the way, most heterosexual people also worry about being rejected for various reasons if they are authentic in their expressions. Some of those worries may even be connected to the fear of being perceived as LGBTQ, and so they stifle their expressions.) Unfortunately, we sometimes find ourselves in situations where it is not safe to be ourselves. At times, we have to weigh the pros and cons of disclosing our identities or being outwardly authentic. We may decide that a given environment is not safe for us to completely express our authentic selves. These are legitimate concerns, and we need to make decisions about protecting our safety in a conscientious manner.

All of this decision making about expressing ourselves authentically or concealing our true selves takes enormous mental energy. Sometimes we don't even recognize the amount of energy that we may be expending in this kind of mental activity. To ensure our well-being, we must find and help create safe environments for ourselves and others. If an environment is unsafe for LGBTQ people to express their authentic selves, then that environment is not safe for anyone.

Being honest and living authentically expresses hope for the future. Hope plays an important role in how satisfied we are with our life. When we are hopeful, we believe that we have some influence over the quality of our lives and the ability to achieve our goals, even if there are challenges or obstacles in our path.

MY INHERITANCE: 34-YEAR-OLD GAY MAN FROM INDIANA

From my perspective, the greatest asset in being gay is the freedom to live outside of society's norms and view society from an outsider's perspective. I found this difference before I found others like me. I admitted my difference, found authenticity, and embraced my self. I count that step of authenticity and being honest with myself and others as my inheritance as a gay man. Men before me made that step, and I give thanks for their example. Men after me will make that step, and I hope to be an admirable example for them. And some will not find the strength to do so, and my heart hurts for those unable to live out their inheritance. While my sexuality is not the entirety of my being, it influences my attractions to others, and therefore is a large contributor to my perception of my world. If I were heterosexual, I would be a very different person than I am; and I like myself too much to want to be a different person. Being gay automatically brings with it countless prejudices, oppression, and inequality, which only serves to increase my sense of resilience because I am comfortable with who I am despite these negatives. I am hopeful and confident that one day sexuality will no longer be burdened with the stigma attached to it today and that everyone, regardless of their sexual identity, will enjoy equality and respect under the law and from society at large. I consider myself honored to be counted among the countless brave gay souls who went before me to evolve my world to where it is today, as well as those talented and brilliant souls who filled our world with art, music, literature, poetry, invention, history, creativity, beauty, and compassion.

EXERCISES AND ACTIVITIES FOR REFLECTION AND PRACTICE

Being your authentic self in the world can take some reflection and practice. We suggest some exercises and prompts that might help you think about your authentic life. Some people will enjoy just reading and thinking about these questions. Others will enjoy writing their answers on the computer or in a journal. And still others may want to talk about these questions with friends or family. You may want to answer or undertake some of the exercises but not others. Whatever you choose is fine.

1. Reflect on the question "Who am I?" Write a short description of yourself. Include in the description and underline three to five words that describe the essence or core of your authentic self.
2. Have you discovered your authentic style? What are you wearing when you look in the mirror and say, "I like what I see!"? What aspects of your physical self-expression feel authentic and true? Are there certain types of dress or style that would better express your authentic self?
3. What are the things that you like about yourself? What qualities do you have that make you proud or feel satisfying to you? Ask your

friends what they like about you. Write a list of these qualities in a journal. You may want to review the list on occasion.

4. Make a collage, a drawing, or a sculpture that expresses who you are and what you value about yourself. Or make a picture slide show or documentary that reflects your values and authentic self.

5. Many people feel that they have a sense of purpose in their life—a mission. What do you see as your mission in life? Write a "mission statement" that expresses what you want your life to be about.

6. Write an essay for yourself that celebrates your identities. What do you think are important things about you that you and others should celebrate? What does this essay reveal to you about your deepest-held values and priorities for your authentic life?

7. How does your LGBTQ identity play a part in your sense of who you are or your core values? How does your LGBTQ identity play a role in the expression of your authentic self?

8. Reflect on how you spent your time yesterday. Did your day reflect at least one of your core values or something that is important to you? If you were living according to your own values and priorities, what would a day in your life look like? What would you do? Who would you spend time with? What activities would you engage in? For you, what does it mean to live your life to the fullest? How does your LGBTQ identity play a role in this?

3

SELF-AWARENESS, PERSONAL INSIGHT, AND GROWTH

"Deepening my insight into myself has led to positive developments in my life."

"Know thyself!" Living an authentic life requires self-awareness and insight. Self-awareness comes when we pay attention to our thoughts and feelings. We use this information to make meaning out of our experiences. Insights come from our meaning-making. Insights about our patterns of behaving and thinking, about our relationships and how they work, and about our families and society all come from observations of ourselves and the world around us. Personal growth results from understanding more about our thoughts and feelings as a result of our self-awareness and insights. Our experiences of personal growth may include increased feelings of inner strength and confidence, compassion for others, and finding and embracing our talents. These types of growth lead to an increased sense of well-being.

For many people, the coming-out process is filled with self-awareness, insight, and personal growth.[1] The insights that we develop are part of the complex thinking that is required to figure out and express our identities as LGBTQ people. Complex thinking includes questioning assumptions about and rethinking the norms or rules of our society that others may take for granted. Our awareness and insights facilitate our growth in many areas of our lives, including the development of positive LGBTQ identities.

While we discuss each of these qualities (awareness, insight, and growth) separately, they are very closely related to each other. Often we cannot talk about one of these qualities without talking about the others. A "gay, queer, transgender" person, 26, living in Louisiana, lays out the interrelated processes as, "My identity is positive because of the process I had to go through: gaining good introspective abilities, getting to know myself well, learning how to stand up for myself, and being true to who I am. These things have given me confidence in my ability to do things in my life, even when others say it's not possible. I believe in me."

In the coming-out process, and beyond, LGBTQ people face unique challenges and have unique opportunities in our lives. How we face these challenges and take advantage of these opportunities helps to facilitate the growth of our life skills, knowledge, and wisdom. We may articulate some of our insights and understandings in spiritual terms or in a more general philosophy of life. Some of the outcomes of our personal growth (such as compassion and authenticity) are the subjects of other chapters in this book. In this sense, this chapter describes a foundational set of skills that help us develop into our authentic selves and enhance our well-being.

SELF-AWARENESS

For many LGBTQ people, the development of our sexual or gender identities starts with an awareness of being somehow "different" from the people around us. Unlike most members of racial, ethnic, and some religious communities, LGBTQ people rarely grow up surrounded by people who also identify as LGBTQ and who can act as role models for developing positive LGBTQ identities. In contrast, most racial, ethnic, and religious identities have family and community support readily available. LGBTQ-identified people have to become aware of our difference and then search for support and role models (we talk about connecting to and finding support in the LGBTQ community, for example, in chapter 9). This process is challenging and provides opportunities for insights and personal growth.

During the coming-out process, LGBTQ folks become more aware of our thoughts and feelings. We may first experience ourselves as "being different" or "my body on the outside does not fit with who I am on the inside." In "being different," most of us have to come to a new understanding of ourselves, separate from the understanding of ourselves that we have in relation to our family and community. If these thoughts and feelings are perceived as threatening or scary, we may initially reject them or push them out of our consciousness. Self-awareness increases when we pay attention to and acknowledge these thoughts and feelings. This is an important step toward self-acceptance and cultivating a positive identity.

Say that, for instance, we become aware of specific feelings of attraction to someone of the same sex. Acknowledging those feelings and accepting them as a part of ourselves is an important step in our self-awareness journey. This is the case for a 28-year-old gay man from Virginia:

> I think embracing same-sex attractions is like making a very special discovery about yourself. This discovery represents the honesty of understanding yourself. So, in a manner of speaking, embracing my homosexuality suggests that I understand myself. I can live my life true to who I am as an individual. Understanding yourself and allowing yourself to be who you truly are is something that can be embraced. I had to work through societal expectations to understand myself, so I feel like I truly have a better understanding of who I am, the damaging effect of societal expectations, and how I fit into society. It also helps me to be better at virtually everything I do.

As suggested by the story above, becoming aware that you are attracted to members of the same sex, or, for others, that your gender identity is different from how others see you, requires paying attention to your feelings. The process of "waking up" is an important part of healthy psychological development for everyone and leads to a more positive overall experience of life.[2]

Being self-aware is a skill and a strength. It transforms our experience of ourselves. A 22-year-old "Transgendered FTM (not-Female) Genderqueer" person living in Ohio tells the following story of self-discovery and acceptance:

I am glad that I now identify as transgender. It was a shift for me that came with letting myself actually consider how °I° feel about myself, rather than only ever considering how everyone else wanted me to be. It is a level of openness I hadn't had with myself before a couple of years ago. It is amazing how much more in tune I have been, not only with my gender identity, but with my opinions about pretty much everything. The acceptance of it being okay to reject everyone's expectations in terms of gender have also made it easier for me to share my opinions about other things. I'm no longer so much of that quiet 'lump' that never says anything . . . I don't know if this new attitude would go away if I would happen to stop identifying as transgender for some reason, but it came with the shift in thinking. I think any form of acknowledging that your own gender identity may not match what the world says, and being able to say that to people, demonstrates a level of self-acceptance and openness. It is an indication that you have really thought about how you feel about both yourself and society's rules. And deciding to change your gender to align with your identity shows a commitment, strength, and determination that not many people would be able to show.

Many of us live our lives doing what we believe is expected of us instead of being consciously aware of our feelings and desires. There are many rewards for paying attention to and acknowledging our thoughts and feelings. However, if what we feel and want is different from our family's expectations or society's rules, it takes a serious commitment to self-awareness to allow ourselves the freedom to explore new paths in life. A bisexual man, 36, from Toronto, Canada, shares the story of his self-discovery:

The journey of sexual growth and discovery I've gone through has been wonderful, and being bisexual is a big part of that. If I had been straight, I probably would have been less motivated to become sexually self-aware because I could have just done what everybody else was doing, without really thinking about it, without questioning. I also find that most bisexuals I meet have gone through similar journeys and are more articulate about their sexuality and often more self-aware in general than my community of straight friends.

Research suggests that identifying as LGBTQ may motivate our thinking more complexly about ourselves.[3] *Cognitive complexity* is a term used to describe people's ability to think multidimensionally, often perceiving and analyzing subtle clues that others miss. People high in cognitive complexity are flexible and creative in their thinking, putting information together in unique or novel ways. LGBTQ identities provide opportunities for a better understanding of ourselves and ourselves in relation to others. To increase our self-awareness, we must become aware of what we are experiencing in the present moment. With this awareness, we may come to new understandings that allow us to discover our unique place in the world and novel ways of being ourselves and interacting with others. Personal insight comes as we make this discovery.

PERSONAL INSIGHT

Once we are aware of our thoughts and feelings, we can begin to make meaning of our experiences. That is, we can observe ourselves and those around us and put the puzzle pieces together in ways that give us new understandings. This understanding of ourselves and others is what we mean by insight. Developing our skills of awareness and insight also improves our overall emotional and social intelligence.[4] *Emotional intelligence* is "the awareness of and ability to manage one's emotions in a healthy and productive manner."[5] *Social intelligence* is the "ability to act wisely in social relations."[6] The abilities to manage our emotions and interact positively with others are important to our overall sense of well-being.[7]

Personal insight allows us to interpret and understand the feelings or thoughts we have become aware of; that is, it helps us to connect the dots. For example, a lesbian from Hawaii in her late 20s tells about her sudden insight into her sexual identity: "I had crushes on my counselors at summer camp when I was a kid, but I never really thought about it until I got to college and was attracted to the woman in the dorm room next to mine. When I thought about it, I realized, duh, I'm a lesbian. Since then my life has made a lot more sense." Insight, achieved by taking time to acknowledge and reflect on our thoughts and feelings and experiences, helps us make sense of our lives.

Sometimes insight is referred to as *introspection*. Introspection simply means looking inside ourselves and trying to figure out what we think or feel and why. Introspection can lead us to understand how and why we may find ourselves living "outside the box" of social rules that our culture has handed us. A 24-year-old gay man living in Washington, D.C., for example, links his introspection to his identity and self-understanding: "Being an out gay man allows you to understand yourself in a unique way, because you have had to go through an intense period of introspection."

For many, the hard work of self-discovery of their LGBTQ identities is a source of personal strength. They are creating their own identity instead of following the herd. A young gay man from Kansas tells how he gains strength from exploring and creating his own identity: "Coming to terms with being gay, admitting that I am not in the majority, has given me a greater depth of self-knowledge—knowing that I have explored my own identity and not simply inherited one from society and the media. This makes me a stronger person." A lesbian, 40, from Arkansas finds that this process develops her confidence: "Another positive aspect is that being gay encourages one to really search within for self-understanding and acceptance. Since society is largely not very supportive of gays or gay rights, a gay person needs to find inner sources of strength and confidence."

Psychologists refer to the process of having insight about our life as *ego development*.[8] For instance, we realize that there is more than one answer to life's Big Questions and more than one way to live a meaningful life. These insights lead us to a more expansive view of the world and a more compassionate view of others.

Struggling to make meaning out of an outsider status helps us develop our ego strength.[9] People who have ego strength are more likely to critically examine the *oughts* and *shoulds* of social norms. A 48-year-old gay man living in Georgia realizes the empowerment that comes with his "outsider" status: "By being, or being considered, an outsider, I have had to question, explore, and create my own reality. Although frequently difficult, I believe this has allowed me to seek meaning beyond the usual prescribed social constructs. The coming-out process is one of self-discovery. My own degree of openness about my life empowers me."

The insights we have about life as a result of our LGBTQ identities can be complex. Or they may be a simple conclusion that sets the tone for our future. A 60-year-old transgender "heterosexual woman" from

Illinois shares her insightfully simple conclusion about life: "Realizing that I am transgender has made me think very hard about who I am and how I want to live. It has forced me to understand that there are many ways to lead a satisfying life and that no one way is the right way. I have learned that life is truly precious." This type of insight about life can be one key to a sense of well-being.

PERSONAL GROWTH

The personal growth that comes from cultivating self-awareness and insight is important in the personal journeys of LGBTQ individuals. A sense of growth, of changing in positive ways, and of moving forward in our lives enhances our well-being.[10] Cultivating positive LGBTQ identities is an important part of our personal growth and well-being. Claiming our strengths, having self-confidence, acting compassionately toward others, and finding and embracing our own particular talents are important parts of our growth processes that may be linked to insights we have as part of our LGBTQ identities.

Many LGBTQ people tell us that they grow stronger as they engage the processes of self-reflection and introspection about their identities. Coming out may be a big part of growing into strong, courageous, and resilient people. A 26-year-old gay man living in Alaska compares himself to his straight peers and notes the importance of his coming out process to his growth as a person:

> Ultimately, coming out has provided me with growth experiences and a subsequent level of maturity greater than my peers seem to have. I have had unique opportunities to grow in so many different ways. My peers seem to have a hard time being in touch with their feelings. I seem to know more about who I am and what I want. I think that comes in large part from my experiences with coming out.

Confidence in ourselves grows as a result of our insights about our identities. Personal growth and the development of inner strengths are part of and facilitate our identity development. For example, a 22-year-old "genderqueer" living in Texas comes to the conclusion that "I am stronger and wiser because of my struggles as a transgender individual and am able to help others in their own life struggles, whatever they may be." Meeting and overcoming challenges from a variety of sources, internal and external, contributes to a sense of personal growth and resilience. A 25-year-old lesbian living in New York provides an example of the growth and subsequent strength that came from dealing with her status as "other":

> Being an 'other' in our society gives me greater perspective and understanding of other marginalized groups. This, coupled with the whole coming-out process, has given me a greater sense of self. I've gained so much strength and self-confidence since identifying as a lesbian. As an 'other,' you must either be courageous and stand up for who you are or constantly live with inner conflict and lying. In a nutshell, being a lesbian has made me a stronger person.

While individuation (becoming our own person, separate from our family of origin) is considered to be a part of healthy development for all people, for LGBTQ people the process may help us to develop cognitive complexity as mentioned earlier in this chapter. A 44-year-old bisexual woman living in Ohio recognizes this skill: "I feel that the process of accepting my same- and other-sex attractions made me think more complexly about myself and others." When we use these cognitive complexity skills to increase our understanding of ourselves and others, we are able to make our own choices about how we want to live our lives. Making choices that are consistent with our self-knowledge, insights, and values is both the *result of* and *results in* personal growth.

The skills that we learn and practice during the coming-out process and the strengths that we develop as a result may also enhance other parts of our lives. A 38-year-old "lesbian, woman-loving-woman" living in Connecticut explains how she finds her inner strength valuable in all aspects of her life: "Coming out made me stronger—I had to learn self-respect, self-love, confidence. I believe in me, I know I can be whatever I want. I know I can be strong. Only when I came out did I find peace—inner peace. It makes me strong, resilient. I take that with me every day, everywhere I go."

Over time, the choice to affirm ourselves and live authentically helps us to grow and develop our abilities and our strengths. Feeling like we have some control over our lives is important to our sense of well-being.

A 26-year-old lesbian from Maryland recognizes the importance of this self-efficacy:

> Being a lesbian and dealing with homophobia (internal and external) has made me a stronger, deeper person. I really like the way my life is going, and it feels like I actually have more control over it (as much as possible) than what I hear straight people around me say about their own lives. They feel like they have to do certain things a certain way. I feel like I can look at my life more clearly and choose my life course.

Acknowledging and building our strengths does not mean that we are oblivious to our weaknesses and challenges. Personal growth comes from seeing *"the good, the bad, and the ugly."* When we are able to see the basic goodness of our identities as LGBTQ people, then we have additional strength and energy to deal honestly with "the bad and the ugly" without losing our perspective about our basic worth and dignity.

Having personal confidence and strength helps us to deal with the challenges we face in life.[11] Self-acceptance includes accepting that our limitations are part of our humanity. Inner strength helps us find ways to be effectual without having to be perfect. For a 27-year-old lesbian from Illinois, the insight and self-awareness that led to coming out also led to other self-insights and personal growth: "Accepting myself as a lesbian has made me better able to see all aspects of myself. I have been able to accept all the good and not-so-good parts of myself and learn to work with what I have been given."

With increased insight into ourselves, our relationships, and the world around us, we are better able to choose to take actions that are consistent with who we are and what we value. As Maya Angelou says, "When we know better, we do better." Cultivating our self-awareness and insight helps us to know ourselves and others better and thus make choices and decisions that are consistent with that knowledge. *Doing better* encompasses many possible actions. Depending on the individual, doing better could mean protecting the environment, repairing a relationship, getting out of debt, going back to school, working for social justice, or helping to build homes for people in need. Many of us have stories of how the strength derived from our LGBTQ identities leads us to have more compassion and empathy for others. A strong sense of self is integral to this process. (We talk more about the themes of empathy and compassion in chapter 7.)

An openness and willingness to engage in self-reflection and introspection is an important prerequisite to personal growth. Personal growth requires that we take responsibility for creating a life that is meaningful and authentic. In that sense, who we are is not static but is an outgrowth or consequence of all of the choices we make about our lives. The process of discovering and choosing to fully accept and celebrate our LGBTQ identities unfolds in the daily choices and decisions that we make.

Our values can be significantly influenced by our LGBTQ identities (in addition to other family and cultural influences). For example, a 60-year-old gay man from Virginia offers a story about how his "gay eyes" have helped to shape his values:

> Another reason to celebrate being gay is how it has shaped my values. In addition to the values of individuals' rights and worth, seeing the world through 'gay eyes' has affected how I see and value liberty, justice, fairness, humanism, and beauty. Much of the beauty in the world has been more open to me as a result of my being more in touch with my own sexuality and sensuality.

Growing and developing our LGBTQ identities can also mean developing our unique talents and abilities. Finding a way to use these talents to benefit ourselves and others reconfirms our positive sense of self. A 52-year-old gay man living in Oregon, for example, attributes his talents to his "gay spirit": "I believe every talent I have comes from my gay soul. My music, art, athletic performance, my intellect, my emotional strength and ability to love all arise from my gay spirit."

We integrate our thoughts, feelings, and behaviors when we act in ways that are consistent with our insights and unique perspective on the world. It is powerful, as the Greeks may well have suspected, to "know thyself." A 35-year-old gay man from Ohio gives us an example of how his self-knowledge and understanding leads to self-empowerment:

> I have less worry about what others think, less stress, and I'm more able to craft my own life self-consciously. I really feel like my being gay and accepting it has unleashed some of the creativity I was sitting on out of fear. I am more free to examine my assumptions about myself, about oth-

ers, and about society, rather than uncritically accepting them. I feel that my being gay and working through the meanings of that has really opened up my life and caused me to be much more suspicious of authority and therefore more flexible. My happiness is so much less dependent on what others think. I feel like I've self-consciously opted out of a lot of the BS that society teaches us to care about.

QUESTIONING ASSUMPTIONS (AND AUTHORITY)

As the quote above (and others) point out, questioning assumptions and challenging the rules and norms of society may lead to unique insights and perspectives. Developing cognitive complexity enhances our ability to question the norms of society or what is often called the status quo. Many of us have seen the bumper sticker "Question Authority." That command may have a special resonance with LGBTQ people.

A gay man from Wyoming explains why it is reasonable for LGBTQ people to question social norms: "Because homosexuality is often taboo—even recently illegal—yet good in my experience, it has made me examine other social and legal bans and decide for myself whether they are good or bad. Whether the topic is marijuana or Christianity, being gay has given me a critical eye and sharp sense of irony in recognizing the double standards of society."

LGBTQ-identified people are what we might call "bicultural."[12] That is, we experience living in both a heterosexual male/female culture and an LGBTQ culture. Psychologist Laura Brown explains that this experience creates "different ways of knowing and understanding oneself and one's reality."[13] This process challenges us to think, question, and think again. A 19-year-old Latino "lesbian queer" college student from California explains her version of this think, question, and think again process:

> The most important thing about being gay to me is that it forced me to question my assumptions about gender and relationships. By nature, I tend not to question the status quo—it's a tendency I'm trying to combat Until I fell in love with a female friend, I had always assumed I would grow up, get married to a man, and have children, simply because that was what everyone did, right? My parents, liberal in many other ways, encouraged this. I never for a moment thought that there were other options.

Once I realized that girls could like girls—and that, in fact, I liked girls—I started questioning other things—first about sexuality, then gender . . . it was as though a sort of gateway had been opened. If this thing that I had considered a fundamental truth of life wasn't required, what else was I assuming? In short, it's made me more aware, and because of this awareness I've become involved in social justice organizations attempting to eliminate white supremacist and patriarchal ideals as well as homophobia.

LGBTQ people commonly tell us that personal growth has come from personal insights that follow claiming their LGBTQ identities. They ask themselves questions like, "If I am different in this way, how else might I be different?" Or "If I'm bisexual, what does that mean about how masculine (or feminine) I am?" A 40-year-old "bisexual queer" man from England gives this version of a self-question-and-answer process:

When I came out to myself as bisexual, my attitude was 'I assumed until now that I was straight, but now I realize I am bisexual; I wonder what other assumptions I have had that are also incorrect?' So I started to reconsider my views on many issues. I have found this reconsideration of assumptions to be fascinating. I guess you could say that coming out to myself as bisexual made me less dogmatic in my views on many issues and has also given me an interest in many topics that used to be uninteresting to me when I identified as straight. Another thing I have noticed over the years is that if a person is a member of an oppressed group, then they might have an attitude of 'I'm oppressed, therefore I am incapable of oppressing others,' but I can see that they hold prejudices toward other groups. By being bisexual, I sometimes experience prejudice from straight people and sometimes experience prejudice from gay people. It was this experience that made me realize that being oppressed is no guarantee that you won't oppress others. This realization caused me to become more aware of my own prejudices toward other groups, which I feel has been an important part of growth and self-discovery.

SPIRITUAL GROWTH

Some people describe the process of being aware, having insight, and experiencing growth as a spiritual experience. *Spirituality* may be defined as "having [coherent] beliefs about the meaning of life that shape

[your] conduct and provide comfort."[14] For some LGBTQ people, spirituality helps to provide or guide our sense of the meaning or purpose of our life. Our spirituality may provide a sense of being a part of something larger than ourselves. We may recognize our connection or interdependence with other people and with nature through our spirituality. Some of us express our feelings and beliefs about this transcendent part of ourselves through religious practices.[15] Others of us will express our spirituality in any number of positive or transformational ways, from walking in the woods to artistic and creative expressions to doing good deeds.

Some LGBTQ people may describe their experience of claiming their identity as part of their spiritual journey. A 37-year-old gay man from Pennsylvania exemplifies this journey:

> Another positive aspect of this journey has been my own need to examine my religious and spiritual upbringing as my gay identity developed and consider what role spirituality would play for me as a gay man. I think that all the experiences of struggle that often constitute the development of a gay identity become a positive—in knowing self, in building relationships built on authenticity and congruence, in learning to stand with others and for oneself. Finally, I would say that a positive of being gay has been that in my search to find meaning in my own life, I have met and become connected to so many wonderful people (who self-identify in many ways regarding sexual orientation) who want to address this issue in their own lives and in society. All of this is part of my spiritual growth.

For some LGBTQ individuals, our identities have spiritual meanings that may be linked to general or specific religious beliefs. We have heard simple statements, such as "God made me this way" or "this is a gift from God." Others have elaborated on this theme. For example, a 40-year-old "Transgender FTM straight man" from Michigan tells us, "I am experiencing true spiritual growth now because I have come closer to understanding God is the one that created me in His image." A bisexual man, 30, from Alabama concurs, "I've become stronger in my [Christian] faith because I have had to decide to follow the spirit rather than heterosexist rules."

Some LGBTQ people speak of their identification with Native American "two-spirit" people and the strength that implies. Throughout human history certain cultures have recognized the exceptional spirituality of *queer* people by elevating them to special roles as spiritual leaders and healers in the society.[16] A "Two-Spirit transwoman" from Colorado, 61, explains the spiritual meaning of this tradition: "I was created in the image of The Creator. I am a mirror to both the male energy and the female energy. I can see from my experiences and insights why Two-Spirit people were chosen as healers and protectors of our souls in the history of my (tribal) nation." A 55-year-old "indigenous person" (Native American) gay man from Arizona explains his identification as two-spirit as putting him in touch with both the "masculine and feminine parts of my soul." He elaborates, "I feel like I can bridge the great gender divide as well as the gay/straight divide as a two-spirit person. I have a richer vision of the world. I can experience my spirit more authentically and see other people's spirits more clearly."

WHAT IS RIGHT FOR ME? 35-YEAR-OLD "TRANSSEXUAL TRANSMAN" FROM ENGLAND

Having a Transgender identity has forced me to think extensively about who I am; what is important to me; how I think and feel about myself. This remains at times a very painful process, but it has also enabled me to grow, mature, and become more self-aware. It has forced me to think about stereotyping, about being and feeling marginalized, and has increased my empathy with others in minority groups or on the margins. I think I have become a more sensitive, thoughtful, compassionate person. Because I can't easily answer some basic questions or categorize myself like other people seem to be able to do with ease or without even knowing that this might be an issue (i.e., which box on the questionnaire do I tick? the M or F, as there usually is no third option), I have been forced to interpret and reinterpret myself and my values. Because I often don't feel I can follow 'the norm,' I question 'what is right?,' 'what is right for me?' I spend much time thinking about masculine/feminine labels, stereotypes, boundaries. I try to occupy both spaces as much as I can. I try not to limit myself either through societal convention, but also, which is much harder, through my own negative stereotypes. In this way I become a more rounded, whole, and inclusive person. I have to find answers to how can I negate my female body, but still be a sincere feminist? It has made me a more political person. It has made me a strong, courageous human being. It also makes me feel frightened and weak and despairing; it confronts me with immovable boundaries and the realization of my own limits. These are certainly not enjoyable and fun experiences, but important and ultimately positive ones. Contemplating changing my sex/physical appearance for me is also questioning how much I can/should change my destiny. What do I have to accept and learn to live with, learn to love, and what can or should I change? I am forced to think about 'the other' in me and how I learn to live and integrate this into my life/my body. If I wasn't transsexual I don't think I would be thinking about these issues, because they are difficult and painful and I think I would just be too lazy. Ultimately, though, they are important questions, not just for individuals, but for society and beyond.

EXERCISES AND ACTIVITIES FOR REFLECTION AND PRACTICE

Self-awareness and insight are skills that we can cultivate. The more open we are to self-examination, self-reflection, and feedback from trusted others (who love and honor our authentic selves), the more awareness and insight we can develop. The ability to ask tough questions of ourselves and to answer as honestly as possible is a skill that many LGBTQ-identified individuals practice while coming out and learning to live more authentic lives. It's a skill that helps us to know all parts of ourselves better. The following exercises and activities are designed to help you to reflect on and further develop your self-awareness and insight.

Exercise 1: Self-Awareness and Insight

Take some quiet time to reflect on these questions. You may wish to write your answers in your journal. Or talk about them with a friend.

1. Do you remember some of the first times you were aware of feeling different about your gender identity or romantic/sexual attractions? How old were you? Where were you?

2. Was there a specific event that triggered this awareness? What feelings accompanied this awareness?
3. What insights did you have about those feelings?
4. When did you first identify those feelings as part of an LGBTQ identity?
5. What personal insights do you feel you have gained from your identity as LGBTQ?
6. How have those insights helped you to achieve or develop a positive sense of self?
7. How can you share those insights with others to help them achieve a positive sense of self?

Exercise 2: A Dream Journal[17]

For some of us, dreams can be a rich source of information about ourselves. Paying attention to what we dream about can help us gain insight into our experiences and our creative potential for solving problems and living meaningful lives. For one week, keep a dream journal. When you wake up, try to remember your dreams and write them down.

Describe the people, places, and events that occurred. What are the two or three most important or memorable elements of your dream? These elements might be the location, an object, a person, or an event. Note your thoughts and feelings as you experienced them in the dream. How does your dream relate to things happening in your life?

Exercise 3: Assessing Personal Growth

Examining the choices we make may help us evaluate whether or not we are becoming the kind of person we want to be and creating the kind of life that is meaningful to us. When we are aware of the choices we are making and have insight into the consequences of those choices, then we are able to choose differently if we so desire. Answer the following questions as honestly as you can. You may wish to write the answers in your journal.

1. What have you done better in your life since claiming your LGBTQ identity (or identities)?

2. What are you doing that gives you a sense of purpose or meaning? What aspects of your life bring you satisfaction?

3. What choices could you make that would help you in the process of becoming your authentic self or that would increase your sense of purpose and meaning? What new activity or even small action could you take that would be consistent with your sense of purpose?

Exercise 4: Exploring Your Spirituality[18]

Consider the following questions. You may wish to write answers in your journal. Or discuss these questions and answers with a friend.

1. What role does spirituality play in your general sense of well-being?
2. How do you define spiritual well-being?
3. How has your LGBTQ identity (or identities) shaped your ideas about spirituality and spiritual well-being?
4. Who are your spiritual role models or influences? Do you have positive role models that support your LGBTQ identity as part of your spirituality and spiritual growth? If not, how might you locate a source of positive support for your "gay spirit"?

4

FREEDOM TO CREATE NEW RULES

"I live beyond the binaries."

"Be a man!" "Act like a lady!" We've probably heard these and similar orders when we were acting in a way that failed to meet someone else's expectations. For many LGBTQ-identified folks, there is something stifling, perplexing, or even downright offensive in these commands. One of the positive outcomes of the strengths of self-awareness, insight, and authenticity is that these resources enable us, if we so choose, to create a way of living beyond the binaries—that is, beyond being "a man *or* a woman" and beyond being "gay *or* straight."[1] Our strengths allow us to express ourselves in a variety of ways in different roles in our lives.

Social norms and cultural rules dictate that everyone must fit into one of two boxes—either female or male.[2] Some people refer to this as "the sex binary." For most people, their legally assigned sex is determined by the outward appearance of their genitals when they are born. They are immediately labeled "a boy" or "a girl" (thanks to modern technology, sometimes this happens even before birth). If a person is born intersexed (with "ambiguous" genitalia), medical professionals engage in all sorts of attempts to make the person fit into one of the two boxes that must be checked on the birth certificate: female or male.[3] The birth certificate also records a legal name. This name typically gives other people, even if they can't see us, a big clue as to whether we are considered to be male or female.

Making people "fit" doesn't end there. While some people would argue that our actions, behaviors, and even thoughts are biologically determined, society doesn't seem to want to take any chances. From the minute we are born, we are treated differently based on whether we are labeled a boy or girl.[4] We are taught in subtle and not-so-subtle ways how to act out specific gender roles based on our assigned sex. *Gender roles* refer to the scripts or sets of rules that tell us how to behave as "a man" or "a woman." The ways that men are supposed to act are labeled "masculine," and the ways that women are supposed to act are labeled "feminine."[5]

Breaking the established gender rules and making up our own is usually frowned upon. For example, when we watch home videos, we may see adults laughing at a boy dressed as a woman or a girl dressed as a man. This may be quickly followed by comments indicating that while this is all good fun, the child needs to change quickly and conform to social norms so that people don't get "the wrong idea." The clothes we wear, the jobs we hold, the hobbies we engage in, the feelings we express—these and many other things are governed by our assigned sex and the accompanying rules about feminine versus masculine behavior.

We acknowledge that refusing to conform to rigid gender rules can be challenging when we have to deal with people who are not very open-minded or who feel threatened by anyone who is different from them. On the other hand, conforming to rigid gender rules may be costly, because they are not necessarily healthy for us, either physically or mentally.

Anyone who lives outside of, or beyond this binary of choices is creating new space and forging a new trail. A 57-year-old "FTM" talks about the lessons of living "between the male/female binary": "Being not 'one or the other' but being 'both and' is a place of privilege that allows me insights into the complexities of gender identities and gender relationships that many people do not experience. Being transgender presents a challenge to accepted thinking and stereotypes and encourages us all to examine our own prejudices and blinkered views."

A sense of freedom and strength may accompany living outside the rigid gender or sex boxes.[6] Indeed, the very act of claiming LGBTQ identities violates the rules. This violation, of course, opens up space for creating new rules for gender roles and relationships. Creating and learning new ways of acting beyond the binaries may enhance our relationships and serve as a positive model that will help our children to flourish also. Another way to break the rules is by rejecting or subverting all of the conventional labels (including straight, male, female, and even LGBTQ). Taking this stance can be a positive act of self-determination.

BREAKING THE RULES AND CREATING NEW ONES

Re-creating the rules about sex and gender can be an important step toward well-being for all people, regardless of sexual or gender identities.[7] We may suffer less psychological distress and enjoy greater well-being when we are able to express ourselves more authentically (as discussed in chapter 2). In other words, we may develop our skills and increase our well-being through the process of breaking the prescribed rules and roles. For example, one research study indicates that the more flexible the gay men in the study were in their gender roles, the less angry, anxious, and depressed they felt.[8] Another study indicates that lesbians who created their own understanding of their gender identity, which includes breaking and re-creating the rules, developed "increased meaning-making capacity."[9] In short, we are more well-rounded individuals when we have a greater repertoire of responses and a greater range of expressions available to us.

Indeed, going beyond the binaries may allow LGBTQ people to create more authentic expressions of ourselves and our feelings, especially within our intimate relationships. This may in turn lead to more satisfying relationships and lives.[10] A 45-year-old bisexual queer woman living in Missouri eloquently explains the benefits of pushing against the limits of conventional gender rules:

> I believe that being bisexual and queer gives me the opportunity to discern how I want to interact with each individual that comes into my life, not based on categories that often are used as limits, but do not need to be. I believe that our society already has too many rules and limits on intimacy, on love, on sharing, on human interaction. Gay or straight,

masculine or feminine are unnecessary limits in defining ourselves. I have made many choices in my life that push against or obliterate these rules and limitations. I would not have it any other way. It has made me a more compassionate and wise person, I think.

Breaking the mold and stepping outside the conventional rules creates a sense of freedom to define oneself. As a 57-year-old lesbian from Colorado who has been out since she was a teenager puts it, "I suppose one of the positive aspects is that there are no real structures in place for 'how to be a gay woman' as there are for heterosexuals in this culture. It's pretty much make it up as you go along." As a result of breaking the mold, LGBTQ people can mix it up, creating new genders and sexes, new rules, and new ways of acting and interacting. Everything can be mashed up in exciting, unique, and challenging ways.

LGBTQ individuals report that once they step outside the box, they feel free to be creative and express themselves in a broader range of ways. For example, a 58-year-old "man-loving-man" from North Carolina writes, "Being gay expands my creative side and opens me to various nontraditional roles. This expands my life." Many of us who identify as LGBTQ find that by embracing our identities we can be ourselves and be authentic with fewer constraints. Sometimes that may mean embracing "acting like a man" or "acting like a lady," but with a critical consciousness that these are created, chosen roles.

For many gay men, freedom from gender roles may include the freedom to express themselves emotionally, something that "real men" are typically taught to suppress and avoid. A gay man, 52, from Rhode Island provides an example of embracing both his feminine and masculine sides: "My identity has allowed me to expand my worldview. I have developed an expanded appreciation for the arts (opera, ballet, painting, symphony), travel, other cultures, the finer aspects of life. I have been able to explore my 'feminine' and 'masculine' sides more."

Living a bicultural life helps LGBTQ people become more flexible in our understanding of gender and sex and to see that life is full of possibilities.[11] A gay man, 30, from Texas tells about the connection between his identity and feeling free to express himself more fully:

Being gay has given me the ability to move outside of the limiting heterosexual and gender-based box that heterosexual men reside in. That is, I am allowed to have interests that are not gender-stereotyped; I am more free to express myself in terms of behaviors and emotions—I do not have to monitor as closely what I do, think, and feel to make sure it conforms to what it means to be a 'real man.'

While some gay men may "look all manly," they can still appreciate the gender flexibility they have discovered as part of their gay identity. For example, a gay man, 37, from North Carolina shares this story about his role flexibility:

I believe that I have a more flexible view of what it means to be a man and to be a man in a relationship. This openness to less rigid views of masculinity (and by extension, femininity) allows me to help others see opportunities for growth and new solutions that they may not have been able to see. It also allows me to live less rigidly masculine roles. I look like a bear and can act out the typical male role. But because I cast off that role in my coming out, I have the freedom to be sensitive or artistic or girly or whatever else I want to be in my life.

For many lesbians, the sense of freedom from conventional gender roles may include feelings of independence, confidence, and strength. These feelings are often denied women within traditional gender-role socialization. A general sense of this freedom is illustrated by a lesbian, 68, living in Kentucky:

Being lesbian gives me the freedom to be who I am, rather than trying to figure out how to be the woman society expects me to be. That is very empowering! It seems to clarify the ways I interact with the world. It makes the patriarchal world stand out in stark contrast as limiting to women (and I might add, men too). It feels like a totally normal way to 'be in the world' and I wonder why everyone isn't as lucky as I am.

While the "tough guy" image is celebrated, generally the "tough woman" is not. However, for some women, their lesbian identity allows them the freedom to be and act strong. A lesbian, 30 years old and living in Iowa, explicitly recognizes and acts out this freedom: "I can play (to some extent) by different rules in life. That is, I can be a strong, tough, aggressive woman, because I have already broken a major rule by being a lesbian." A similar sense of strength is expressed by a lesbian, 32, from

Utah who explains the impact of her identity on her workplace actions: "Because I am not personally bound by gender expectations, I have no qualms about being assertive at work. I never worry that my actions might be considered unladylike."

Identifying with both feminine and masculine qualities and being able to express both comfortably can have positive benefits at work as well as in personal relationships. Being able to express both our so-called masculine and feminine qualities gives us more flexibility in our actions. The more flexible we are in our responses, the better able we are to be effective in a wide range of situations. As a business practice, this flexibility may have benefits for the bottom line. A 57-year-old transgender man from Oregon explains the benefits of his gender flexibility in his managerial role,

> My identification with and possession of female values and attitudes is very beneficial. I was an upper-level manager in my career, and extremely successful, to a very large degree, because I practiced inclusiveness and openness, while shunning power plays and destructive competitiveness. The other male managers didn't know how or just couldn't let themselves be open to cooperation and change. That limited them.

QUEERING THE RULES

Queer has traditionally been used as word that describes something that is "strange or odd from a conventional viewpoint; unusually different."[12] Embracing our queer identity (whether we use that word instead of or in addition to LGBT) signals a challenge to the conventional rules. A 50-year-old "bisexual queer" person from Ontario, Canada, tells how living outside the conventional rules provides important opportunities for exploring life: "We have the potential to think outside the box, to live in nontraditional relationship structures, to throw off traditional gender roles, and to live a life that is full of a variety of experiences that are not open to most straight people."

Queer identity embraces creating new rules. Queer identity celebrates playing an active role in creating a positive life. A "lesbian queer" living in New Mexico, 36 years old, illustrates this broad-ranging embrace of queer identity and its positive benefits:

I chose to primarily identify as queer (instead of simply lesbian) because to me it implies a challenge of the status quo, not only in regard to 'traditional' heteronormative sexuality, but because it allows me to challenge other perceptions as well—race, class, religion, etc. Queer implies a willingness to be active, to be visible, to be political, to be radical. I love the fact that my partner and I are not trapped by stereotyped gender roles in our relationship. Either of us can be vulnerable or strong at any time. We can cry and we can comfort each other without any extra emotional weirdness. She is more mechanical than I am, and I like to cook. But in terms of our friends' and families' perceptions of us, I can't see that they assign either of us to a particularly butch/femme male/female dichotomy. I like to challenge other people's boundaries and expectations in this way and in the way that I dress.

Not being confined by the ordinary rules frees us to think more complexly about ourselves and others (cognitive complexity is discussed in chapter 3 also). A 27-year-old "queer who happens to love someone of the same gender" from Minnesota expresses how the freedom of queer identity facilitates the recognition of life's complexities:

The most positive aspects of being bisexual—or what I identify as being queer—is that you get to express all intimate parts of yourself; you're not boxed in by one set of expectations or confined to a specific label/role. I love myself and I love expressing myself, and it is freeing to live a life that affirms those two things. Being bisexual/queer helps me to affirm all parts of myself in this world that constantly tells us all that we must 'choose.' Not everything is cut-and-dried or black and white, and I believe that one's sexuality is not something that can be explained, experienced, and fulfilled in such plain, restrictive terms. Humans are very complex, and thus human sexualities are complex and determined by various factors. Furthermore, the modes of identification and expression are also just as complex and diverse.

Queering how we live recognizes different ways of being and acting. Queer identity can challenge gender rules and the mandate to act out heterosexual roles (a mandate sometimes referred to as *compulsory heterosexuality*).[13] It also challenges the idea that *if* we are not straight, *then* we must be gay or lesbian. A 48-year-old "queer, bisexual, pansexual" man from Washington State explains that his rejection of these assumptions is rooted in his queer identity:

> Being bi and queer gives me an opportunity to be attracted to and enter into physical and/or emotional relationships with both men and women. I find this a very positive aspect of my life. This flexibility gives me insights into how multiple types of relationships operate and makes me feel as if I have myself grounded in multiple positions. Since this is an open and ambiguous space, it also is a place of power and change; it operates outside the gay/straight binary, so it allows me more opportunities to work/think/experience things out of the typical, socially constructed, two opposite poles of identity recognized by society. This space, since it is neither and both, also means that a person is often stigmatized by both. While at first this might seem to be negative, it helps me to see the negativity of the stigma directed at both groups. From a resiliency and strengths perspective this skill helps me to operate in both, as well as other spaces, in a stronger and more flexible way. Being grounded in a space that challenges binary constructions of sexuality helps me challenge other binary categories like race, ethnicity, class, sex, gender, etc. . . . I like to think this skill makes me a better person overall as I challenge systems of power, privilege, and oppression.

NEW RELATIONSHIP SCRIPTS

In intimate relationships, the social convention is "one man and one woman." (We'll talk more about freedom to explore sexuality and relationships in chapter 5.) The sex box that is checked on your birth certificate prescribes that your intimate partner should have the *other* sex box checked. The relationship that is formed includes strict expectations and instructions for behaviors and roles to be fulfilled by each member of the couple. Queering the rules (and the boxes) dispenses with these automatic prescriptions.

When LGBTQ people go beyond traditional gender roles and sex binaries, when we think outside the box, we have an opportunity to create new scripts for our lives, including our relationships. These new scripts hold the possibility of being more flexible and making relationships stronger. For example, a 43-year-old lesbian living in Texas recognizes how her relationship with a same-sex partner nullifies the conventional scripts: "There are no gender limitations on anything—we do what we do best and what we like to do. For example—I'm very feminine and my partner is more masculine. However, I'm physically stronger and I don't mind getting dirty. So I do the heavier work. It's great to not have to fall into society's predefined categories based on our appearance." Writing a new script for our lives and relationships can be a very positive and healthy step in enhancing our well-being.

In our current culture, sex determines which gender role we are assigned and socialized into. Living outside of the assumed heterosexual male or heterosexual female assignments creates a space for exploring new ways of expressing what it is to be male or female, or just to be human. The insights into the authentic self that often accompany LGBTQ identities can be a resource for expressing ways of being that don't match the assigned roles. Breaking free of these constraints is an indication of our self-determination. The ability to exercise self-determination can be a source of strength in all areas of life.

A 23-year-old woman living in New Hampshire, for example, locates her sense of self-determination in her lesbian and queer identities:

Being a lesbian allows me to explore gender roles outside of the traditional female role. I feel that my gender is more fluid not only since I've started to identify as queer, but more so since I've been in a same-sex relationship. I can be either masculine or feminine, or neither or both or something else. I can choose to cook dinner and clean without feeling like I'm being forced into that domestic role by the opposite sex. I can also explore traditionally male-dominated fields without having to feel unfeminine.

For some LGBTQ individuals, part of the freedom from gender role expectations includes freedom from pressures to follow the traditional heterosexual script of getting married and having children. Having less outside pressure allows some LGBTQ folks to appreciate and carefully evaluate their options for having children. A lesbian, 40, from Michigan appreciates the lack of pressure from her parents such that "we chose to have children instead of being expected to have children. My parents put the pressure for grandchildren on my straight sisters, not me (but they were happy when my partner and I had a child)." A 30-year-old gay man from Canada feels free from the "heterosexual timeline": "I am free to form my own definition of a relationship. And this relationship does not have to follow a heterosexual timeline of marriage and children, etc. Both are legal options here, so my partner and I can choose what and when it is right for us."

Without the limits of heterosexual rules, LGBTQ people may also have a greater range of choices about how to raise their children. A gay man, 37, living in California reflects that "there is less pressure on gay men to have children and as such, the decision for a gay man to have or not to have children may involve a healthier process. Then how we raise a child is also a process of choosing how best to raise a child, not how are we expected to raise a child." A lesbian, 30, from New York contrasts her perception of her experience raising a child to that of the straight women she observes: "Being lesbian provides you with a wonderful community of people who tend to think outside the box and approach problems creatively. It allows for a range of gender expression (though I, personally, am as straight looking as we come!). Being lesbian allows us to choose to have children and how to raise children in ways not claimed by straight women. Straight women seem to have to follow some set of rules; lesbians can be more creative in allowing our children to grow and experience a lot of different things."

For a lot of LGBTQ parents, the positive strengths of their identity set a good example for their children.[14] Their children are provided with more flexibility and choices to discover themselves and act authentically instead of following the conventional scripts. For example, a "gay man-loving-man" from Vermont, 49, explains how his identity benefits his sons:

I'm able to see how hollow the 'real man' and 'real woman' ideals are. That's really positive for me. My sons have turned out to be completely outside the mold for straight men. They don't like sports—they see how it is a system of discrimination against differently abled persons—they don't care about cars, stereo equipment, and all the other stereotypical interests for men. That's very satisfying for me, because most of the cultural norms for men in the United States are harmful to others: women, minorities, and anyone with differences. I think my being gay played a large role in opening their worlds.

LGBTQ identities allow us to claim our strengths, and for parents this is an important part of being a positive role model for their children. A gay woman from South Carolina, 36, examines how her identity influences her actions and the lessons she wants her daughter to learn:

> Because I am quite an assertive, competent, and accomplished woman, it is easier to be with another woman who is not threatened by that. When in a heterosexual relationship, I always felt that I had to make myself smaller (metaphorically and physically) in order to be seen as feminine. Now I have no qualms about being assertive and strong. I live as a full person. I want our daughter to grow up knowing that she can be anything, and be strong, and I think it is great to be an example for her.

Parents model relationship styles for their children. For a 45-year-old lesbian living in California with her partner and raising a daughter, modeling both "openness about gender roles" and a positive relationship style is important:

> As a lesbian, I have had the opportunity (and challenge) to carve out my own identity, separate from the pressures on heterosexual women. I feel like I know who I am, and it doesn't come from the outside. That's definitely a product of being 'other.' I have an unbelievably wonderful relationship with my partner. We communicate very well and very honestly about our parenting differences and work things out well. And our child benefits from our openness about gender roles. She is becoming who SHE wants to be—femme or not, straight or lesbian or bi, physical or bookish, whatever. We don't have preconceptions about money and power and share power well in our relationship. I have more freedom to love my body and wear what I want to and not have to conform to heteronormative standards of beauty. Our daughter can see all of this and know the possibilities for her life are limitless.

THE POSITIVE "NO LABEL"

Some LGBTQ people, while understanding how we fit into the alphabet of identities, may choose to reject labels altogether. Or we may combine and create elaborate labels that feel more accurate, such as "pansexual queer man" or "dyke transman." For some, the problematic issue is that with labels come scripts, with scripts come expectations, and with those expectations come constraints. A 24-year-old "queer bi" woman from California, although she labels herself, refuses to label other people unless they have labeled themselves first: "I think the best part about being bi is that I see beyond people's gender and see them as individuals and love them for the person they may be. Although I call myself bi, I am not too concerned with labels and I find that freeing. It doesn't matter to me how others label themselves, and I don't place labels on people that they didn't place on themselves first." For this person and many others, there is power in labels. This woman respects the right of others to claim that power for themselves.

For some people, adopting any sexual identity label, including the label bisexual, implies a binary ("monosexual" vs. "bisexual"). As human beings we are complex, and our experiences cannot be fully captured in any single label.[15] For example, a 22-year-old recent college graduate from Wisconsin comments on how inaccurate and overly simplistic *bisexual* is as a label for her experience: "I make the distinction that just because I use the term 'bi,' which implies 'two,' that I do not believe that there are just two genders. I believe there is a continuum for gender just as there is for sexuality. I would rather not limit myself with a label." A 32-year-old woman from New York expresses a similar reservation about labels and their constraints: "I think the positive things about my identity relate to the fluidity of my identity. I question basic assumptions about relationships and sexuality. I actually prefer the term queer because bi implies a gender binary and is not inclusive of trans/ genderqueer people, and I am attracted to people across the gender spectrum."

For some people, this fluidity and flexibility of identity can be experienced as a foundation for establishing a solid sense of self. A person from Florida, who did not endorse any of the sexual or gender identity choices on the survey, explains, "I don't have to worry that I will be attracted to 'the wrong sex.' My sexuality can be fluid. I don't have to be straight or gay or bi. My gender can be fluid. I don't have to be masculine or feminine. I can just be me."

For some, the notion of the *sex binary*, that we must label ourselves male or female, is not applicable or is too limiting. Our culture in the United States, and in most other cultures in the world, is very sex conscious. We are not referring to sexual behavior here, although that applies too. We are referring to the forced choice on innumerable forms that have just two boxes: male and female. There are no "I'll decide later," "not applicable," "either," or "both" options. Choosing one or the other is enforced by social norms (and, we might add, by various institutions). Nowhere is this two-category system better illustrated than in public restrooms in the United States. We must choose: men or women (or any number of variations on the theme: gents or ladies, studs or fillies, etc.). In fact, most times the words are not even present, just pictures—a *man* in pants and a *woman* in a dress. We are taught to recognize these symbols as different (that is, we are expected to know that *men don't wear dresses* and women do) and we are expected to go into the correct room that matches our assigned (and perceived) sex.

Some transgender-identified individuals describe their sex as well as their gender as "fluid." Others simply find the female/male binary too limiting of their self-expression. As a transgender-identified person, 32, from Vancouver, Canada, simply states, "To be bound as a 'woman' or 'man' is stifling." Further exploring this theme, embracing the possibilities of being neither a man nor a woman is a positive strength for a 20-year-old transgender college student:

> I can't be 'too feminine to be a man' or 'too masculine to be a woman' because I'm neither of those two! I don't need to worry about whether my behavior suits my gender because there are no set rules for 'transgender' the way there are for 'man' and 'woman.' To me, these are all positive things.

AN OPEN IDENTITY: 25-YEAR-OLD "QUEER BISEXUAL" FROM NEW JERSEY

The first positive thing about being bi that comes to mind is feeling as though I am simply being myself. Imagining myself identifying as heterosexual doesn't feel right, but neither does identifying as a lesbian, and even the term 'bisexual' feels a little off because of its limited nature in dichotomizing gender identity. Having a more open sexual identity makes me feel more at home with myself and open to other people. Similar to that, I feel as though it's a pretty positive thing to be able to be open to any gender identity and open to any kind of love or relationships I might find myself in. Living in a very heteronormative world often restricts the kinds of relationships people are expected to have and limits them to stereotypes. I have also experienced 'the gay world' as having stereotypes and gay versions of many of the same restrictions in the heterosexual realm. I feel like being queer is so much more broad and open to a much wider spectrum of relationships and the types of emotions and loves you can experience with different people. It isn't about sex, either, it's about appreciating people on many different levels and loving people more for who they really are rather than the stereotype they try to live up to.

EXERCISES AND ACTIVITIES FOR REFLECTION AND PRACTICE

The rules and scripts that prescribe how to act as a "man" or "woman" are so pervasive in our culture that many times we don't even notice them or how they affect us. It can be difficult to stand outside of our own experience and really see how the world we are enveloped in impacts us. Here are a couple of exercises designed to help you gain some perspective on the influence of gender-role socialization in your life.

Exercise 1: An Alien Encounter[16]

Imagine that a spaceship lands in your backyard and two friendly aliens emerge. The first alien asks you for lessons on how to be an "average man." What are the top five lessons that you would give? The second alien asks you for instruction on how to be an "average woman." What are the top five lessons that you would give?

What do these lessons say about how you view the "average man" or "average woman"? What if a third alien asked you for the top five lessons on how to act like a "human being" – what would those lessons be? How would your answers differ? What can the average man and average woman learn from the human being?

Exercise 2: Gender Role Analysis[17]

In your journal, reflect on the following questions.

1. List the messages you have been taught about "masculinity" and "femininity." You might try completing these sentences:

   A "good" man does _____. A "good" woman does _____.
   A "good" woman thinks _____? A "good" man thinks _____.
   A "good" man feels _____. A "good" woman feels _____.

2. What are the sources of these messages about what makes a "good" man or woman? Family members? Peers? Schools? Media? Church? Other sources?

3. How has your LGBTQ identity affected your ideas about these messages?

4. What limitations or even potential harm do these messages cause you and others?

5. How do you think you express your gender in ways that are different from or that are the same as non-LGBTQ people? Which of the gender messages or scripts that you identified above have you resisted or would like to resist? Are there any rules or messages that you enjoy embracing as part of your identity?

6. How do you think your gender identity impacts your sense of self? Do you think people are surprised by the way you act or the strengths that you have?

5

STRONGER EMOTIONAL CONNECTIONS WITH OTHERS

"Sharing my true self brings me closer to the people I love."

"Is she 'family'?" "Is he cool?" These are just a few of the many questions that we ask each other when we are trying to figure out who around us will be *cool* with our LGBTQ identities. Sometimes these questions are asked just as a matter of general information. Sometimes they are asked to assess our safety around others. And sometimes the questions are asked to try to figure out whether to show interest in the other person and signal that we want to be friends. Connecting with others is an important aspect of our positive well-being.

Many of the LGBTQ people we interviewed note that their identity helps them to make stronger emotional connections with other people. Sharing any part of our identities is a revealing act, but sharing our sexual or gender identities may seem even more revealing and intimate (as compared to, for example, sharing information about our work identity). The act of trust involved in this reveal creates an opportunity for mutual sharing and closer connections.

Our emotional connections may be with straight men and women as well as members of the LGBTQ community. These connections may be with members of our family of origin or our chosen family.[1] The connections may be with our intimate partner or our children.[2]

We may feel strong connections with our friends. Creating a support network is important for all people but may hold a special significance for LGBTQ people.[3] A 26-year-old gay man clearly states his perception of this significance: "I feel that one of the most positive things about being a gay man is the ability we have to create our own extended families. We shelter those seeking refuge from families who no longer want them to be a part of them. I know this is something that all adults, gay or straight, are able to do, but as a gay man, it's more important."

Humans are social beings. One of the basic needs we have is connecting with others and feeling like we belong.[4] Relational psychologists have identified five good things about healthy connections with others.[5] First, connecting to others gives us zest or a sense of vibrancy. Second, this energy empowers us to act in positive ways. Third, good relationships increase our self-knowledge and our knowledge of others. Fourth, when others attend to us and validate our experiences, our sense of self-worth increases. Fifth, healthy connections generate a kind of momentum that leads us to seek other healthy connections and extend our compassion and empathy.

A close relationship involves a strong emotional connection and a type of interdependence that allows both people to give and receive support. Close relationships may include shared activities or experiences, empathetic sharing, compassion, and a feeling of attachment. Having a close relationship with another person can help us feel valued and contribute to our sense of purpose in life. In short, positive relationships with others help to add meaning to our lives.[6]

For LGBTQ people, our identities may enhance our relationships with others in a variety of ways (whether we reveal our identity or not). This includes our one-on-one relationships as well as our relationships in small networks of people with whom we have an established, ongoing relationship (our family, friends, or coworkers, for example). Our relationship with our intimate partner may also be enhanced. (We save talking about our relationship to the broader LGBTQ community for chapter 9.) All of these relationships, when close and supportive, enhance our sense of connection, belonging, and well-being.

SHARING BRINGS US CLOSER

For LGBTQ people, support from family and friends is important to a sense of satisfaction with our lives.[7] Support from straight friends and family helps us cope with minority stress and helps us to maintain positive relationships outside the LGBTQ community.[8] People who identify as allies often describe the moment their LGBTQ friend or family member discloses their identity as an important, positive event in the relationship and as a turning point in their deciding to become allies.[9]

Sharing our lives gives us a sense of closeness with others in our life. It raises our sense of self-worth and enhances our lives in numerous ways. Sharing information about ourselves is an act of trust and takes courage. Hopefully most of the time, the person we are sharing with will honor that trust sharing and honesty of their own. Being worthy of someone's trust also feels good. It brings people closer together. A 22-year-old "fluid bisexual" from Pennsylvania gives an example of this process: "It's been something positive for me to share my sexual identity with people I trust quite a bit. I would say in the majority of cases it's brought me closer to friends or coworkers who know, because they also view it as an act of trust."

Sometimes sharing comes in a quiet, private conversation. People can share thoughts and feelings at one point in time or the conversation may take place over days, weeks, months, or years. Other times, sharing takes place in a small group or a large crowd. Maybe a person talks about their same-sex partner or spouse at a party with many others overhearing or reveals during a public introduction that their chosen name is Andrea instead of Andy. These not-so-private conversations can lead others to feel a moment of connection. That moment may foster closer relationships in the future.

The workplace is one environment where informal sharing may take place. Having supportive coworkers and meaningful relationships at work increases our satisfaction with our lives.[10] A 30-year-old "queer, gay man" from Michigan notes that his coworkers are an important part of his social network: "Being open about my sexuality at work affords me the opportunity to have normal discussions with coworkers about our 'spouses' and not feel the need to try to hide anything or lie about what plans for time off or the weekend may be. It's just normal to share these things, and it feels supportive to be included in all of the conversations."

Sharing openly may help to put others at ease and make them more likely to share with us. For example, a gay man, 44, from New York writes that his gay identity facilitates his relationships with straight men by allowing them to share more openly: "I like how I've served as a bridge for some straight men who are attracted to my masculinity, yet I am not competitive with them in certain ways. They often feel free to open up to me because I'll understand and yet not put them down for being fallible or vulnerable as their straight male friends might."

Even for a person who doesn't disclose their LGBTQ identity in every situation or to every person, being able to emotionally connect with others is a positive life skill. A gay man, 62, from Nevada discusses how his gay identity facilitates his close relationships with others in a variety of situations, even when he is not out to some people:

> I think that as a gay man I am more sensitive to the feelings of others, and although I am not out to many of my friends and acquaintances, I think I have a special relationship with most of them, which would not be as close if I were straight. Although I am a masculine man and not in any way obviously or stereotypically gay, I am able to express my feelings when appropriate and in return, receive honest and sincere responses. Although I cannot speak for all gay men, I believe that friendships between gay men are more honest and genuine. I have also experienced a deeper and more meaningful friendship with straight male friends when all the bravado and macho talk are ditched and conversations are about mutual interests, such as politics, religion, history, science, etc., and about the human condition. I enjoy this openness and feel that it is mostly a result of my gay identity.

This example illustrates how, when not hampered by the pressure to conform to society's rules and stereotypes about masculinity by restricting one's emotions, gay men are freed to have emotionally intimate connections with other men.[11]

CONNECTING WITH OTHERS

Living outside the typical rules about gender and relationships may help LGBTQ people connect with others. For example, living outside of strict heterosexual gender roles may allow lesbians to be "one of the guys" or allow a gay man to befriend a straight woman without the sexual expectations of traditional heterosexual female/male relationships. A 39-year-old gay man from South Carolina enjoys the freedom from expectations: "Living outside of many of society's expectations for male-female interactions, gay men are free to have closer, nonsexual friendships with women (lesbian or heterosexual)." A lesbian, 43, from Montana feels a connection with straight men in a way that straight women might not: "I tend to get along well with straight men because they see me as an ally. Some men actually treat me with more respect than they treat straight women. Of course I call them on that and don't let them talk disrespectfully about women. I think they take that better from me because I'm their buddy."

Creating an integrated social world that includes both heterosexual allies and LGBTQ people may enhance well-being.[12] A 32-year-old lesbian living in upstate New York tells how simply living honestly expands her network of friends and helps her form connections with many different people:

> There are many unexpectedly positive things about being a lesbian. My partner and I have made an agreement that as we encountered new people in our lives, we would merely act the way that felt natural, in other words, act like ourselves. We are not segregated into the gay community by any stretch of the imagination, but are lucky to have a very diversified group of friends counting straight and gay couples, gay and straight singles, minorities, with a huge range of ages among them. I believe, in fact, that my group of friends is more diverse specifically because I am a lesbian.

Some LGBTQ people describe their opportunities to have deeper connections with friends, regardless of sex or sexual identity. One gay man, 35, from West Virginia talks about the role of his openness in feeling close connections with others: "Another positive thing about being completely open about my sexuality is that I have much closer friendships with both straight men and women than most other people I know. I know that if someone chooses to be one of my friends, they are doing it because they accept who I am completely without any reservations." The story is similar for a lesbian, 48, living in Massachusetts:

> I am able to have close friendships with both straight and gay men without any concerns or confusion over whether there is any sexual component

to our relationships. I am also able to have close friendships with both straight and gay women, because straight women seem unconcerned about my sexuality and other gay women are obviously comfortable with it. Before I came out, I had a hard time establishing close friendships with other women. All of my closest friends at that time were men. Since coming out, I've been able to continue having close friendships with men while also developing similarly close friendships with women.

Being more open to expressing and sharing our feelings may facilitate increased closeness in relationships. These relationships may be more intimate than typical friendships. A "bi femme" from Toronto, Canada, 28, explains how her bisexual identity removes some of the boundaries in friendships and facilitates closeness:

> I believe that being bisexual allows me to form deep bonds, deeper than the typical bonds of friendship, with people of both sexes. I have discussed this topic at length with many of my straight friends. Many of them seem to feel as if they cannot form deep bonds with friends of the same sex. They seem to feel there is an invisible line where friendship ends and, should they go beyond that line, they would be faced with difficult questions surrounding their sexual identity and orientation. I feel that being bisexual allows me to love my friends deeply without being fearful of loving them 'too much.'

The process of developing LGBTQ identities may help to heighten awareness of how others around us are feeling or what they are expressing. For some this heightened awareness is especially true in their interactions with other LGBTQ people (for a similar theme, see chapter 9). An 18-year-old gay woman going to college in California sees herself as being more "tuned in" to others, especially her gay friends:

> I truly do think I am more in tune with what is happening in my life and the world around me than are my straight peers. I 'read' my gay friends, and they me, far more easily than my straight friends (who seem generally unaware—not unsupportive, but a bit lost). Being gay gives me a very strong tie to other gay people, men and women, because we understand what it is like to be in a place that we weren't raised to be in, and dealing with the reality that has been placed before us (for better or for worse).

Living outside of the social rules and expectations may account for the reputation that some LGBTQ folks have for "talking about anything; nothing is off-limits." This freedom to talk about *anything* brings a feeling of closeness with friends, especially LGBTQ friends. A 35-year-old gay man from Pennsylvania points to open communication with his friends as a primary reason for why he feels close with them:

> For me there is nothing better than the closeness that male friends, especially gay friends, share with each other. I am not necessarily talking about sex either. There are things my gay friends and I discuss regularly that my straight friends would never dream about discussing with their straight friends. Gays and lesbians seem to be more open about how they feel, think, and live than straight people are. Maybe it comes from decades of being pushed around or in the closet, but with every step out of the closet, gay people seem to open up more and be more honest about themselves both to themselves and any other person that plays a significant role in their life.

Self-disclosure, sharing one's feelings without censoring, creates emotional intimacy between people. We are happier when we develop and maintain this level of closeness in relationships with at least one or two people in our lives.[13] For LGBTQ people, their identities may play a role in developing these close relationships.

FAMILY OF ORIGIN

Family of origin, the family we are born into or grew up in, can be a source of support and a source of stress, sometimes in the same sentence! Some members of our original family (hopefully *all*) are joyfully supportive of us; others may not be so supportive. We often make up stories in our heads about how our family of origin will react to our LGBTQ identities. Some of those stories come true. Many are fearful exaggerations. And sometimes we are just plain surprised by the amount of support we receive when we do come out to our families of origin.[14] For example, a gay man, 50 and living in Washington State, who recently came out to his parents, tells us about the surprising result: "When I came out, I was the first person to be totally shocked at how supportive my parents were and still are at the age of 75 and 81; they are pretty cool people."

Our family of origin is typically our first close relationship. When we are young, we depend on our parents or caregivers to protect and nurture us. As we mature, that relationship changes; we create our individual identity and become more interdependent rather than dependent. At that point, closeness with our family becomes more a matter of choice, although our choices are often shaped by our cultural values.

Ideally, our parents and family love us unconditionally and support our identity development. When LGBTQ individuals come out to family, we are deserving of unconditional love and support. However, we know that, at least initially, many LGBTQ folks may experience some negative or lukewarm responses from family of origin.[15] The negative responses tend to lessen over time as family members become more informed and overcome their fears. Most LGBTQ folks eventually feel at least some, and hopefully a lot of support from family members.

For LGBTQ people, working through this growth process of disclosure to family, living authentically, and coping with any less-than-positive responses can, in the end, bring family members closer together. The positive outcome of this process is described by a gay man, 28, living in Ohio:

> My family is the largest positive aspect of my being gay. After coming out to my family, my relationships with my mother, father, and brother have become 100 percent better. I am closer with them than I ever have been in my life. Being completely open about my sexuality has afforded me the opportunity to not feel like I am trying to hide something from the rest of the world, and from myself. By being myself with my family and talking about all the things we talked about after I came out, we worked through a lot of family issues and we all learned to be more honest.

Feeling supported is also important to the quality of relationships between same-sex couples and their families of origin.[16] Family of origin can provide acceptance and create a celebratory atmosphere for relationships. A member of a same-sex couple from Maryland recognizes the meaning of family support for his relationship:

I think that gaining support from our families only serves to strengthen our feelings for each other. It not only lessens our conflicts, but gives us people to turn to. Every relationship has its ups and downs. It is nice to be able to turn to my family and talk to them, and they support not just me but the relationship. They love my partner and want us to be together and be happy. I think they see all that we go through as a gay couple and they want to be even more supportive. That has been really important in our decision to have kids.

POSITIVE RELATIONSHIPS WITH OUR KIDS

Many LGBTQ people have children. Recent studies suggest that approximately one in three lesbians, one in six gay men, and nearly two in five transgender-identified persons are parents (and many more plan to be parents).[17] Positive relationships with children are an especially important aspect of life satisfaction. For LGBTQ people with children, coming out to their children and providing their children with a living example of values such as integrity, authenticity, and inclusiveness are especially meaningful. A 42-year-old gay man living in Florida tells about how his children have benefited from his identity disclosure: "Most important, being out to my children has taught them to respect differences in others and to value each person for who they truly are, not how they look on the outside or who they love. And I hope that it's given them a sense that being 'different' is okay, so that sense can help carry them through the difficult teenage years when being like everyone else can seem so important."

Just as with other relationships, the process of revealing LGBTQ identities to one's children can bring parent and child closer. Claiming LGBTQ identities may change current relationships and offer an opportunity for growth for parents and children. For example, a 58-year-old "transwoman" living in New Mexico discusses the importance of her relationship with her children: "I was fortunate in that my two children loved me enough to be supportive and now they are my best friends. Having family is so important to finding happiness."

Sometimes it may be the child who teaches the parent about the meaning of their new relationship. A 59-year-old "MTF feminine woman" living in Georgia shares this poignant story:

I didn't think I felt any positives about my trans identity; however, I asked my daughter, and she says I wouldn't be the same person to her if I wasn't trans, so she says it's a good thing. Come to think of it, the closeness with my daughter is a positive thing. We both made the effort to make a new relationship, and she especially has been supportive. It has been hard on me to not be a 'father' anymore. But in the end I have grown and changed—for the better, and it's my daughter who pointed that out to me.

Our relationships may be with our own children or with other children within our family. For example, LGBTQ identities may facilitate meaningful relationships with nieces and nephews or grandchildren. A 35-year-old gay woman has a special relationship with the children of her siblings: "As a gay woman with no children, I've become the 'cool aunt' to my nieces and nephews: the one who enjoys spending time with the kids, playing games, and running around, giving them piggyback rides, making holiday decorations, taking them places, teaching them things, and encouraging their interests. This is probably the most rewarding aspect of being gay for me."

CHOSEN FAMILY

As we grow up and become adults, it is not unusual to feel less in common with our original family members and more in common with our close friends. The creation of *families of choice* is an important source of support and a positive aspect of LGBTQ lives. Many LGBTQ folks create families of choice to function as their emotional and physical support network.[18] A lesbian, 52, from Iowa captures the feelings of many: "I feel a freedom to create a family of choice based on love, not biology; to get our emotional needs met is very positive. In the end my family of choice is very supportive of me." A transgender lesbian from Illinois echoes this sentiment: "My family of choice (friends I spend holidays with) is a positive. I rely on them. They rely on me. We can be there for each other in ways my family I grew up in cannot."

Families of choice may include current partners, former partners, children from current and past relationships, and close friends. Chosen families may include some members of our original family and not others. Sometimes we just add to our original families until we have one big extended family of choice. A lesbian, 26, explains her concept of an extended family of choice as "being connected to a chosen family on top of my given family. I have one huge family to support me." A lesbian, 30, living in Washington, D.C., further illustrates why families of choice may be an important supplement to original families: "Many gay people have lots of good friends, good people in their life. We can't choose our family, and most of our family, especially our parents, can't empathize with what it's like to be different than the majority, so we find special people to make up a larger, more diverse family. And this is a good thing."

The importance of family of choice in LGBTQ lives derives from the feelings of love and support that these people provide to us. These are the people who listen to us when we are sad or scared or angry. They are the people who share our joys about our promotions, our new loves, our weddings and unions. They bring us meals when we are ill. They share our grief in times of loss. These are the people we feel closest to and count on, and they count on us. Creating these families of choice supports our well-being. A 42-year-old gay man from Michigan experiences "a real sense of community and support from other gay men and lesbians. They can understand the ups and downs of what it's like to be gay in our society. They can be a surrogate family and share your joys as well as your disappointments." Family of choice may provide the primary emotional support during both stressful and happy times. This can be a great source of comfort, as a 50-year-old lesbian from Tennessee found out while taking care of her aging parent: "I found it to be the lesbians who showed up, my friends who became my family when no one else was around to help with the hard things—physically and emotionally."

Sometimes a person's chosen family does not include anyone from their family of origin. In these cases, a chosen family can provide much needed support. A bisexual woman, 46, from British Columbia, Canada, tells the story of being estranged from her family of origin since the age of 16 (for reasons unrelated to her bisexual identity). To fill that void, she created a close connection to her chosen family:

> I created my 'family' from my friends, some of whom were gay and lesbian, others heterosexual, and we all accepted each other for whoever we were. I was surprised when I first was attracted to a woman that most of

my close friends were very accepting and comfortable with my new relationship, and supported me in it. I think the saying that 'you can choose
your friends but not your family' is fairly indicative of how I view supportive relationships and what I expect of them. Not everyone is open-minded
about sexual orientations or relationships, but if we choose to be around
open-minded, supportive people, the rest doesn't really matter.

Some LGBTQ people talk about the differences between their lives
and those of their siblings or straight friends. LGBTQ people may find
opportunities to create supportive families of choice where straight
people may feel more limited. A 39-year-old gay man from California,
for example, compares his life to that of his straight brother: "I have a
big community of friends and extended family. My brother, who is married with children, is the opposite. When they got married and had kids,
he lost all his friends. He is sad and isolated, and when he is not working
he is doing chores. He says he wants me back as a close family member,
but in truth I get much more love and support from my 'chosen family.'"

FAMILIARITY WITH MY PARTNER

In several chapters in this book we discuss the positive impact of
LGBTQ identities on intimate relationships with our partners.[19] In
this chapter we focus on the positive emotional impact of identifying
as or having experience as the same sex or gender as one's partner,
or sharing a sexual identity. Some people feel that commonalities of
experience or feelings help them relate and bring them closer emotionally to their partner. For example, a 32-year-old married bisexual
man from Maryland talks about enjoying with his wife a shared, similar
taste in men: "Being out with my wife about my identity has brought
us closer. We are in a monogamous marriage, but we will both ogle
the same guys walking by. It may seem trivial, but it's just a fun part
of our relationship to share that. It makes us feel like we understand
each other better."

Having a same-sex partner may create opportunities to share a deeper
emotional connection based on similar experiences or interests. For example, similar experiences based on gender expression or socialization
may form a basis of mutual understanding with a partner. A 40-year-old

gay man living in Louisiana talks about the advantage of this type of "insider knowledge":

> As a gay man, I have insider knowledge about the very group of people I am attracted to. I'm not certain, but it seems that opposite-sex couples spend a considerable amount of time trying to understand each other's motives. I have always had a keen understanding about what I am dealing with, positive or negative, when I am interacting with another man in a friendship or relationship. This saves me a lot of time and energy.

The notion of romantic couples also being best friends may be true for some couples with LGBTQ partners. Comfort with a partner and enjoying similar interests may enhance a relationship. A gay man, 19, living in Wisconsin feels this way about his relationship: "I love spending time with my partner—he's a really wonderful guy, and he makes me feel very good about myself. An advantage to dating a man is that we can do 'guy stuff' together—weight lifting, watching football, wrestling, grilling out, etc. It's like having both a best friend and a lover in the same person." A lesbian, 28, living in Georgia has a similar sentiment about the emotional side of her relationship with her partner: "Another positive thing about being a lesbian is that I am able to not only relate to my partner, but understand her as well. We understand each other's emotions and feelings. This makes it easier to talk. It's like we are best friends."

Some LGBTQ people appreciate the extra sense of familiarity with their partner's body and sexual responses. They feel that this familiarity enhances their emotional and sexual experiences and pleasure (we'll discuss this more in chapter 6). A lesbian, 26, from Wisconsin finds that similarities enhance sexual pleasures: "One of the best things about being a lesbian is feeling love from another woman. I feel women are capable of a deeper, different kind of love, and it is nice to feel the love I send out returned in the same way. Sex with a woman is great because they have the same parts and have a better idea of what feels good. Women are soft and sensual." A 30-year-old "transman" from Rhode Island explains his familiarity with his female partner's feelings and body: "I understand intimately what she is feeling because of my past experience. I can relate to her emotionally and physically. This allows us to be closer than if I had not had that experience and I think this connection is one of the most positive things about my identity and transition."

Communication and understanding are important components of any relationship and increase a feeling of connection with a partner. A 40-year-old lesbian living in Minnesota discusses the role of sex and conversation in a relationship: "The day I first came out to an older lesbian colleague, she said to me about being a lesbian, 'It's not the sex, it's the conversation.' That is the most powerful, satisfying thing, and—not to knock sex!—I have often thought of this and agree with it. It's the conversation, and being fully myself, and fully known. That makes the relationship sexy."

INVESTING IN RELATIONSHIPS: 49-YEAR-OLD "TRANSSEXUAL" FROM CALIFORNIA, MARRIED FOR 16 YEARS

The act of self-disclosure, when done with sensitivity toward the person you are sharing with, is very liberating, and while potentially scary because you risk rejection, it is probably the single most important thing you can do toward mental, emotional, and physical health. Our secrets can damage us. Further, we are investing in our relationships, which is our most important asset, and I think for the most part we are more apt to get as much in return for our risk taking if not more. But as in all investing, our returns vary—and we need to expect some losses. I have found my friends to be much more accepting of me, not less, and we have both gained from the experience. Someday they may come to me with something deep to share, inviting me to give back the gift of acceptance and understanding, further deepening our relationship. Being a transgender person is certainly unique, and seeing things from two different perspectives can be a little unsettling at times, but I wouldn't trade it for 'normalcy' if that's what you would call it. Rather than being weird, I am differently gifted. And I want to use that gift wisely and share it, rather than hide it and waste it.

EXERCISES AND ACTIVITIES FOR REFLECTION AND PRACTICE

The following exercises and activities may help you strengthen your relationships or the bonds between yourself and others.

Exercise 1: Strengthening Our Social Connections

Consider the following questions. You may wish to write your thoughts and feelings in a journal.

1. How has your LGBTQ identity facilitated your emotional connections with others?
2. Who are you out to? Who responded positively and has supported you in your identity development? How has this support contributed to your well-being?
3. Is there someone in your life that you want to come out to? How you might do this? What kind of response would you hope to get from that person?

Exercise 2: Increasing Social Support

Sometimes we don't get support because we are too shy, embarrassed, or afraid to ask for it. We can't assume that people know what kind of support we need or what would be helpful to us. Make a list of supportive statements or activities that you would welcome from a close friend or family member. If you feel comfortable doing so, share this list with the person.

Remember that strengthening connections is a two-way street. Brainstorm some ways that you give support to your friends and family members. You may want to ask these people how you can be more supportive of them. We can learn a lot about each other by having these conversations.

Exercise 3: Families of Choice

Make a list of the members of your chosen family.

What positive impact has your family of choice had on your life? Do they know what they mean to you?

Consider doing one or more of the following activities to strengthen your connection to your family of choice.

1. Write a "gratitude letter" to one of your chosen family members thanking that person for their support. Send it to them or hand-deliver it if possible.

2. Family rituals are important and enhance our sense of well-being.[20] For example, families that share certain meals (say, a Sunday night potluck); enjoy nature activities together (such as taking a Solstice hike or going on a camping trip); or have annual events (maybe going to an LGBTQ Pride march or having a Halloween party), build bonds through positive memories of shared experiences. Make specific plans with your family of choice to engage in at least one ritual event.

3. If you need to build or extend your chosen family, consider "adopting" a supportive grandparent, a cool uncle or aunt, or a sibling who understands you. Think of one positive action you can take this month to start to create or strengthen your chosen family.

Exercise 4: Loving-Kindness Meditation

Strong, healthy relationships require connection to yourself, to others, and to all living beings. Meditation can help us take time to renew that sense of connection. Research has documented that the practice of loving-kindness meditation increases positive emotions such as joy, love, gratitude, contentment, hope, and pride. These positive emotions, in turn, have been shown to increase our self-acceptance and our positive relationships with others (and our physical health!).[21] Even practicing as few as five to seven minutes a day can enhance our social connectedness. Search online for a loving-kindness meditation that fits your style and needs. Try this meditation out for two weeks and see how you feel.

6

FREEDOM TO EXPLORE
RELATIONSHIPS AND SEXUALITY

"I can love who I want and create a satisfying relationship."

"First comes love, then comes marriage, then comes Suzy with the baby carriage." This old adage can take on a whole new look and meaning for LGBTQ folks. The traditional rules for relationships are based on strict gender roles for men and women in heterosexual couples. These rules have loosened up a bit, but they still dominate our culture. (If you don't believe us, try watching a sitcom on television and pay attention to how much of the humor is based on the supposed "war between the sexes" and traditional gender role expectations for heterosexual couples.)[1] However, if a relationship is between two men or two women, or between a transgender person and a man, woman, or another transgender person, then most times "the old rules just don't apply."

If the old rules don't apply, then there is space to create new types of relationships. As a gay man, 39, from Ohio affirms, "There is considerable freedom for a gay couple to communicate, negotiate, and establish their own rules and traditions." For LGBTQ-identified people, the freedom to explore different expressions of our sexuality and different constructions of our intimate relationships can enhance our life satisfaction. Our curiosity about life, relationships, and sexuality, and the ability to embrace novelty and challenges, benefits our relationships and well-being.[2]

Positive intimate relationships play an important role in good mental and physical health.[3] Loving relationships provide us with a sense of connection, purpose, and meaning in life.[4] Having a satisfying sex life is also good for our health and well-being.[5]

Communication is an integral part of creating relationships outside of conventions.[6] Creating a fresh set of relationship rules allows for the expression of personal values within relationships. For example, having an egalitarian relationship may be a valued goal for a couple and is linked to increased satisfaction in relationships. Expressing our values in relationships may include creating new forms of family, without the traditional heterosexual relationship scripts. One lesbian, 45, living in Florida sums it up nicely: "Being a lesbian is positive because it provides the opportunity to create a lot of the rules of life and relationships. I have a freedom to create new types of relationships."

The freedom to explore sexual attractions and expression, to be *sex-positive*, can be a rewarding part of expressing LGBTQ identities. We may realize that there are benefits to having a partner with whom we share sex or gender experiences (see also chapter 5). Or we may experience sexual attractions "beyond sex and gender" that focus instead on valued traits. All of these forms of creating something new are positive and can enhance well-being.

NEW RELATIONSHIP RULES

One of the positive aspects of LGBTQ identities is the freedom to create new rules for relationships. This creativity includes the freedom to "make up the rules as we go along." Negotiating our relationships involves, as psychologist Laura Brown notes, "creating boundaries that will work where none exist from tools that may be only partially suited to the task."[7] The skills that we develop in the process of claiming LGBTQ identities may help us in creating new boundaries, new rules, and ultimately satisfying and successful relationships. We talk about several of these skills, such as insight and empathy, in other chapters in this book.

LGBTQ identities do not conform to the typical rules that society has for us. As a result, many LGBTQ people claim some variation of the theme that we are "not bound by any rules or regulations." A lesbian, 30, living in Connecticut enjoys the freedom of this nonconformity: "There is a built-in separation from societal mainstream norms, which frees me somewhat from having to conform to those norms."

For LGBTQ people, negotiating and creating new relationship rules is a positive part of commitment to an intimate relationship with a partner. A gay man, 40, living in New York explains the positive consequences of this negotiation process: "I think my partner and I have a stronger and more closely examined relationship than many mixed-sex partnerships because we have had to negotiate the rules of our commitment in ways that I think few straight couples do. Our relationship was 'unconventional' to start with, which has given us the opportunity to work on it with a lot of freedom."

LGBTQ people often lack ready-made role models, both for our identities and for our relationships. This can be challenging and also freeing. A 46-year-old gay man living in Kentucky discusses how he and his partner benefit from these challenges:

> Many of the challenges of being a gay man are positive aspects as well. For instance, society provides few role models for gay men in regard to how to date, how to divide household chores, how to interact with 'in-laws,' etc. We have to talk about what our relationship will be like and how to do all of these things. We have to constantly communicate, which can be hard. But it is that communication that brings us closer together.

Without predefined rules for a relationship, LGBTQ people spend time reflecting on our intimate relationships, what they mean, and how to proceed through the joys and challenges of life.

Creating new relational scripts that are free from strict gender roles allows for flexibility. This flexibility in learning to perform and be comfortable in a variety of roles may be helpful to LGBTQ people as we face challenges in life. For example, gender role flexibility is a strength that allows for greater adaptation to the demands of aging and greater flexibility in relationship roles as we grow older.[8] Being willing to engage in behavior that does not conform to strict gender roles is therefore a positive asset that allows individuals to "have a wider repertoire of available coping tools and responses at their disposal as they age."[9] A lesbian, 72, from Washington State talks about how aging affects her relationship with her partner:

> As we get older, my partner and I are having to talk about what each of us is capable of doing. It doesn't matter how we have always done things.

Now, it is who can do what on any given day. It is very positive for us that we have always had to talk about our relationship and negotiate who does what. We've been together for 40 years. We know each other, but we don't know each other as 'old gals.' So we keep learning new things about each other and about ourselves.

A NEW FAMILY STYLE

We find that many LGBTQ folks question traditional gender roles in intimate relationships and actively negotiate their roles within their relationships. Same-sex couples or couples with LGBTQ-identified partners have the opportunity to communicate about who is going to take on what tasks in a partnership. Who is going to take out the trash or fix the car (traditionally the "man's job")? Who is going to do the cooking or the grocery shopping (traditionally "women's work")? For many couples that we have talked with, the answer is whoever likes to do these things, whoever does it best, or whatever feels fair or equitable.

We suspect few people really enjoy or are exceptionally talented at taking out the trash. It's just a necessary chore. The point is that it's not assumed that one person in a relationship will do the task because of their sex or gender. These tasks are open to negotiation and renegotiation from time to time. For example, a 35-year-old gay woman living in Iowa explains how she and her partner share the daily chores: "Simple stuff in our relationship, that I guess opposite-sex couples have a harder time negotiating, is a part of our commitment to each other: we both cook, we both clean the house, I do laundry, my partner cleans the bathroom, I dust, she does dishes more often than not. We both do yard work. We both are willing to buy the tampons."

Most LGBTQ people are in committed relationships. Many LGBTQ people are or are planning to be parents. We know that in most ways, LGBTQ relationships and parenting look a lot like heterosexual relationships and parenting.[10] The "dream" is essentially the same, with a slight variation in some of the characters. A 24-year-old lesbian from Ohio illustrates this: "For a long time I worried that I would never be able to attain the American ideal of husband, wife, two and a half kids, a dog, and a minivan. Now, my partner and I are planning on our own ideal of wife, wife, two kids, a dog, a cat, some chickens, a goat or two, and my trusty '95 Outback."

Forming a family with children outside of the narrow model of "a dad, a mom, and 2.09 children" may allow LGBTQ parents to make different choices about their family formation. There is evidence that LGBTQ parents (especially same-sex couples) are more intentional in their decisions to have children and the makeup of their chosen family for raising their children. A 34-year-old lesbian from Texas lays out the plans that she and her partner have for adding a child to their family:

> There are so many stereotypes that I see some straight couples emulate. (Wives must nag their husbands. Husbands must try to get away from their wives to do fun stuff. Husbands fix stuff. Wives fix dinner.) It is nice to be free to build a relationship without those stereotypes. As my partner and I are currently trying to conceive, it has been interesting to experience the joys of being lesbians in this adventure. I believe that we thought and planned much more carefully about having a child than many of the straight couples we encounter. We have been planning our lives for almost two years in order to surround this child with love and support. We have a very involved and excited dad (sperm donor), with his wife and children, and a host of friends and relatives sharing in the joys and sorrows of our trying to conceive. I believe that our child will benefit greatly from the extended family that we create around him/her as he/she grows up.

Forming families and close intimate partnerships is an important part of the life experience of the vast majority of LGBTQ people. Couple members and their families face challenges and grow together. Facing challenges and adversities together may be valued for the strength it can add to relationships. A 33-year-old lesbian living in Colorado who has been with her wife for eight years shares how they have grown together during their relationship:

> The best thing about being a lesbian is the deep connection and close relationship that I have with my wife. We truly enjoy being with each other. We have an honest relationship. It's like being married to your best friend, and you get to share a sexual relationship too. I see a lot of heterosexual couples that don't actually spend much time together. We do. We want to be with each other, because we have so much fun together. We actually experience life together. I think another positive thing about being a lesbian is that you

have to work through things and grow emotionally. If life doesn't present any challenges, then you don't get to grow as much. It's too easy to take things for granted, such as legal rights, freedom for public displays of affection, and the love/acceptance of your family members and friends. Having to deal with coming out and being out, you learn to appreciate those things that are not guaranteed in life. It is a hard lesson, but I wouldn't trade it. For myself and for my relationship with my wife, it has only served to make us stronger individually and bring us closer together as a couple.

Valuing one's relationship with a partner and the freedom to work through relational rules and roles is important. Although negotiating rules and roles may be done with a partner in any type of relationship, some LGBTQ people see this negotiation process as having uniquely positive consequences for LGBTQ relationships. We may be aware of the more typical roles that we saw in our own families while growing up and consciously reject or reshape those roles. A lesbian, 32, living in Indiana explains how she and her partner consciously reject using her straight, conventional parents as a relationship model and instead embrace a new type of relationship model:

> Being in a relationship with a woman means that my partner is also my best friend. It wasn't that way in my family growing up. My parents didn't seem to be interested in each other. They barely talked. I think two women together are a lot better at communicating and working through problems than a man and a woman. In any kind of same-sex relationship, all the traditional divisions of emotional work and housework and other responsibilities are up for negotiation. In addition, because we are both women, we don't fall into traditional patterns of behavior (one person more masculine/ aggressive/dominant and one more feminine/passive/subordinate) because we are conscious of the ways that these patterns of behavior have oppressed women. When we decided to have a child, we had to really think about it and agree that it was important and what our philosophy was about raising a child. It isn't easy to have a child in a same-sex relationship, so you have to want it more and talk through it more. I think this leads to better parenting and fewer surprises about your relationship.

EQUAL PARTNERS

The word *egalitarian* comes up a lot when talking to LGBTQ people about negotiating relationship rules and family roles. Egalitarian means that both partners have equal power or equal say in a relationship. Women have historically been disadvantaged in heterosexual relationships, especially civil marriages. So creating egalitarian relationships is an important goal for many women (including lesbians, bisexual, transgender, and queer women).[11] Many men (including gay, bisexual, transgender, and queer men) also want egalitarian relationships. In short, many LGBTQ people find that experiencing equality within a couple is an important component of a successful relationship.

We know that, in general, there are few differences between same-sex and heterosexual couples in their levels of couple satisfaction or stability.[12] In other words, couple relationships have lots of similarities, regardless of the sex/gender composition of the partners. But there are a few important differences that may contribute to positive well-being for LGBTQ individuals in relationships. One such difference is the equality of partners in relationships. Research has found that same-sex relationship partners tend to share relationship responsibilities more equally than heterosexual relationship partners.[13] Relationships with a transgender, bisexual, or queer-identified partner may look more like same-sex relationships than typical heterosexual relationships. Thus, LGBTQ relationships may be more likely to reap the benefits of having an egalitarian relationship between partners.[14]

For many, equality starts at home. Sharing household chores and responsibilities is a marker of an egalitarian relationship. For example, a 38-year-old lesbian from Delaware reveals the positive benefits of sharing household responsibilities:

> I have a partner who I understand and communicate with on a deep level. We don't have any weird macho hang-ups about money, status, or control. We deal with our finances easily and don't get hung up on who makes more money or who does more work around the house. We share responsibilities and resources without competition and without having to have one of us be the 'provider' or the 'top dog.'

Communication is a key to achieving an egalitarian relationship. Partners' willingness to discuss relationship values and the "big picture" as well as the details of daily life is important to the sense of equality. This extends to decision making in a relationship. A 35-year-old lesbian living in Pennsylvania sums up how she and her partner approach decisions:

> I am in a committed relationship in which all things are discussed openly and respect for both partners' ideas is central. There are no gender-specific expectations (for example, my partner would never think of sitting on her behind while her partner and the other women clean up after a meal—common issue among the heterosexual couples in my extended family). We both have an equal say in things. We make big decisions together but we also trust each other to make decisions while keeping the other person in mind. We don't have to get 'permission' from the other to do something. In a nutshell, our relationship is equitable.

For some LGBTQ people there is a conscious desire to avoid traditional relationship patterns, including the inequality of partners that is often observed in conventional heterosexual couples. One lesbian, 33, living in Arkansas specifically cites a critical consciousness of the oppression of women within relationships as a motivation for creating an egalitarian relationship: "We don't fall into traditional patterns of behavior because we are conscious of the ways that these patterns of behavior have oppressed women." A 55-year-old lesbian from Oregon elaborates on her freedom from the traditional inequalities that women have faced in heterosexual relationships: "In this culture, with our patriarchal sex roles, the freedom to be in an egalitarian relationship has allowed me to be much more of an independent person—both psychologically and economically—and achieve my own goals in life."

Lesbians are not the only group who value egalitarian relationships. The desire for egalitarian values in relationships applies to people who identify as gay, bisexual, transgender, and queer as well. The insight into the importance of and the high value placed on an equal relationship may come in part from past experience in relationships with both men and women. A bisexual man from Oklahoma, 29, based on his experiences, values equality in all of his relationships:

> Being bisexual provides me with a unique point of view concerning social interactions and intimate relationships. For one, it allows me to contemplate and consider having intimate relationships with both men and women. This has allowed me to open up and explore my own personal

feelings and beliefs about gender roles and societal gender-based expectations. It has also helped me to develop an egalitarian view concerning intimate relationships and the roles that I am willing to explore within them.

Having life experiences as more than one gender or sex may influence the egalitarian relationship values of some. For example, a 37-year-old "MTF heterosexual woman" explains how her experience growing up with male privilege influences her feminist consciousness about relationships:

> I feel like it is an advantage in a relationship to have an understanding of men and how they are socialized (because I was brought up that way). I understand male privilege and its effect on a relationship. At the same time I understand how women are treated in relationships (by men and by society). I am a feminist and want to have an equal partnership. I can only be in a relationship with a man who wants that too.

Modeling an egalitarian relationship for children is important to many LGBTQ parents. For some, equality in a relationship is a basis for modeling respectful interactions. For example, equality and respect are the norm in the relationship of a 36-year-old lesbian from Georgia raising two children with her partner:

> I feel totally equal with my partner. We share everything and all household duties. Our children are being raised in a nurturing, nonjudgmental atmosphere. They can see how we treat each other with respect, and hopefully that shows them that equal relationships are possible. They sometimes comment on how their friends' parents are 'weird' because they treat each other with disrespect.

EXPLORING SEXUAL EXPRESSION

The feeling of freedom to explore our sexual attractions and desires is a positive aspect of LGBTQ identities. All of these identities exist outside of the straight, heterosexual norm. Being outside the norm allows us to explore new expressions of our sexuality, both within and outside of committed relationships. Exploring sexual expression within relationships may enhance intimacy with a partner. A 50-year-old gay man from Hawaii enjoys his sense of sexual freedom: "There is a freedom to explore our sexuality that comes with being openly gay. I have had profound experiences of physical and emotional intimacy with my partner and that, certainly, for me is a positive aspect of being a gay man."

Exploring sexual expression and desire may sometimes be portrayed as though it can only take place outside of committed relationships. But, as many LGBTQ people will attest, it may also take place within a monogamous long-term relationship. A 49-year-old gay man from Illinois who has been in a relationship with his partner for eighteen years feels a freedom to explore sexual desires within his relationship:

> It is positive to discover that I can choose to participate in a sexual lifestyle in accordance with my own desires, rather than feel so much social pressure to adhere to any particular behavioral pattern. For example, I have chosen to be limited to one sexual partner in the context of a monogamous relationship, and that commitment is stronger when it is made freely rather than as an expectation of the greater society. That strong commitment creates a place for me to explore and express my sexual desires freely.

The freedom to explore sexual and emotional intimacy might include being open to a variety of sexual experiences. For example, this freedom might include exploring a range of sexual fantasies, role-playing, open relationships, or polyamory. Some LGBTQ individuals claim a more extensive sexual repertoire that enhances their intimate relationships; they attribute this to their willingness to be open to exploring sexual expressions. This willingness to explore and express may come from a sex-positive attitude. A 21-year-old bisexual man living in California exemplifies this positive attitude: "It is positive to feel free to express all of my sexual desires. I am open to trying new forms of sexuality. I am not scared of my sexuality changing or expanding. I have a greater self-knowledge and the ability to think more critically about sexuality and what it means to be sex positive. I don't feel pressure to conform to the boundaries of any one sexual identity."

Some people think of sexuality and sexual attraction as *fluid*.[15] Sexual expression and attraction are important to our well-being. Fundamental or noticeable changes in how we understand or define our sexuality may lead to opportunities to explore new ways to be sexual. A 24-year-old bisexual man from Ontario, Canada, explains his perception of the differences between gay, straight, and bisexual men in their willingness to explore sexual expressions:

> From my experience: there is typically a reactionary response from gay men (in relation to women) and straight men (in relation to other men) when they are asked if they would consider engaging in sex with members of their unaccustomed sex. "EW, NO! GROSS" or "NO F°CKNG WAY!" are typical responses. I feel these responses are as much a product of the socialization of gay men and straight men in North America as it is an aversion to body differences and sexual experimentation. Bisexual men, as men who are attracted to both sexes and who would, in turn, more openly consider engaging in sexual activity with either sex, may perhaps have a more 'objective' view of sexual activity and the forms and function of the male and female body that a number of gay men and straight men do not. This understanding and appreciation, I find, definitely helps in providing a more positive outlook on body difference and sexual experimentation. As many self-aware bisexual men have consistently pointed out: one's sexual activity (behavior) need not directly inform or dictate one's sexual identity (emotional/cognitive function). This is something I feel more educated bisexual men are more attuned to and can certainly impart to their fellow gay and straight men. The fluidity of bisexuality is certainly something to be praised.

SAME-SEX (SAME-GENDER) SEXUAL UNDERSTANDING

The sexual understanding that comes with being the same gender or sex, or having experience as the same gender or sex as one's sexual partner, may enhance sexual experiences for LGBTQ people (we'll try to give a PG-rated version of this theme!). For some, the feeling of having common experiences or a familiarity on an emotional level enhances sexual connections. For example, an FTM "hetero male," 21, living in Maryland relates to women with a sense of familiarity: "I think dating is easier for me because I know what women think, how they are treated, and how they would like to be treated, what they like to hear, see, do, and so on." For a 38-year-old gay man living in New York, the familiarity is emotional as well as physical: "I'm a man, so it's easier to understand another man than it is to understand someone of the opposite sex. It's easier to read signals, understand motivations, and to know how to pleasure each other in sexual relations."

For others, there is familiarity with a partner's body and sexual responses, or there is firsthand "knowledge of the equipment." This familiarity may enhance sexual experiences and pleasure. A 42-year-old "FTM Transman" from Florida has intimate knowledge of women's bodies based on "years of experience": "Women say I am a better lover because I know female bodies so well. I have years of experience to draw on." Understanding the range of sexual expression with a female partner enhances sexual relationships for a 38-year-old lesbian from Delaware: "It is great to have a partner who understands many of my experiences on a fundamental level because she is also a woman. There is great sex and plenty of romance. Also, there is a lot of wonderful, nonsexual physical affection. We know what women crave because we are women."

Understanding one's own sex or gender may lead to enhanced intimacy in sexual relationships. A lesbian, 35, living in Missouri sees understanding and intimacy as an important component of sexual satisfaction: "The intimacy level is incredible. Women are more intuitive and sensitive toward one another. Sexually, the satisfaction is endless. Knowing how to please your partner and vice versa is just amazing." Another lesbian, 28, from Kansas made an explicit comparison between how she sees relationships between women and relationships between men and women. She explains what she sees as the advantage of relationships between women: "I feel women are capable of a deeper, different kind of love with other women than with men. It is nice to feel the love I send out returned in the same way. Sex with women is great because they have the same parts and have a better idea of what to do than a man would."

ATTRACTION TO THE PERSON

Sexual attraction is often assumed to be based *first* on the sex of the person we are attracted to. Then, the assumption goes, we look at the other characteristics of the person to find out if we like what we see. However, for some people, it is the traits or characteristics of a person that we find attractive *first*, and the sex of the person is not a factor or is a secondary trait. For a bisexual woman from Georgia, 23, the sex of the people she is attracted to is unimportant to her: "It is my experience that when you fall in love with someone, you fall in love with them as a person, not as a body. The body or the sex of the person comes in later, but I don't have to worry about thinking something might be wrong with me just because the person I fall in love with is a man or a woman."

While not strictly limited to those who identify as bisexual or queer, choosing an intimate partner based on characteristics of the person "without regard to the sex of that person" may be more common for those of us with bisexual or queer identities. Human attributes such as personality, moral character, interests, emotional intelligence, and sexual compatibility are valued and prioritized over biological sex or gender expression. This is freeing for a 26-year-old "bisexual, pansexual" living in Massachusetts: "To me, identifying as bisexual is positive because I do not feel restrained to only one certain gender. I can fall in love with the person and the qualities that the person possesses . . . no matter what their anatomy is."

For some people, having a bisexual identity may give them more "options" in their dating life, but more importantly, it allows them to value the other person in a new way. People with a variety of LGBTQ identities have told us that they appreciate the ability to choose an intimate relationship based on the other person's "heart and mind rather than their genitals." As one bisexual-identified 40-year-old woman eloquently describes, "The label 'bisexual' is a misnomer. It's not about sex at all. It's about all the other things about the person that count. I'm lucky I can look at someone and see all of that person as a human being and decide whether I am attracted to them as a person."

OPPORTUNITY TO EXPLORE: 45-YEAR-OLD BISEXUAL FROM PENNSYLVANIA

I believe that being bisexual and queer gives me the opportunity to discern how I want to interact with each individual that comes into my life, not based on categories that often are used as, but do not need to be, limits. I believe that our society already has too many rules and limits on intimacy, on love, on sharing, on human interaction. I have made many choices in my life that push against or obliterate these rules and limitations. I would not have it any other way. It has made me a more compassionate and wise person, I think. Being bisexual could have, I suspect, given me the opportunity to deny my attraction to women and pretend to be straight (and as I teenager I did, for a time) . . . but instead I also saw that being bisexual gave me the opportunity to make a conscious choice to ignore society's heterosexist attitudes and to embrace not only a community of people I might have lost if I'd continued to pretend to be straight, but also to embrace with compassion a more whole sense of my Self. I would have missed out on so many opportunities for good friendship and connection. Being bisexual is a comfort for me; it is what feels normal. Being bisexual also helped me explore my attitudes about what 'being in relationship' means. What committed means. What marriage means when only some can legally take part. What 'open' means. I questioned why we put so much weight on relationships in which we are having sex, when in some cases the physical act of sex is easy, while deep intimacy, trust, connection without sex can be so much more difficult to attain. Again, I have developed an attitude and an understanding about being in relationships that embraces with compassion a whole sense of who I AM, what I desire to be, in relationship with my Self and in relationship with others, and I believe that it was being bisexual that was key to this. I have a unique and open and intimate community of women and men, gay, straight, bi, trans, queer, open, and monogamous. One of the many things that allowed me to feel a deeper and deeper love for the man I am in a committed relationship with is his trust in me, his acceptance of my many friends, his comfort with who I am, completely. I can honestly say that I cannot imagine 'me' as anything other than bisexual.

EXERCISES AND ACTIVITIES FOR REFLECTION AND PRACTICE

The following exercises and activities are created to help you to think about and assess your own relationships and relationship values. When you are clearer about your own beliefs and values, you are more likely to see where you may want to make changes to move you in the direction of achieving your own relational goals. It may be helpful to answer the questions in your journal or to discuss them with a friend or partner.

Exercise 1: Reflecting on Your Relationship Rules

1. Think about the relationships you observed while you were growing up. What relationship rules did you learn from observing these relationships, for example, in your family of origin? What were the gender scripts that people in your family seemed to follow in their relationship?
2. Think about your relationships. Are there ways that you seek to follow the scripts that you learned growing up? Are there ways that you are writing new scripts? How have you gone about creating your own relationship script?
3. Do you feel a sense of egalitarianism or equality in your relationships? If this is a goal for you and your partner, are there ways in which you can have more egalitarianism in your relationship?

Exercise 2: Creating Satisfying Intimate Relationships

Identify a same-sex couple whose relationship you admire. What relationship patterns that you observe appeal to you? If you can, ask them for advice on how to create and maintain a positive and meaningful relationship.

Exercise 3: Reflecting on Sex and Sexual Expression

Few of us have had an entirely sex-positive upbringing. Some of us have been taught to feel shame about our bodies and/or our sexual expressions. Some of us may have endured physical or sexual abuse. Accepting, enjoying, and appreciating our bodies and our sexuality is important to our sense of well-being. Caring lovingly for the body that we have been given for this life is important to our health and well-being. We can move toward this goal by taking stock of where we are now.

Take a moment to think carefully about the societal messages you have received about bodies and sexuality in general. Also, think about the messages about your body and sexuality that you got from your parents and other influential sources.

1. What messages about your body, sex, and sexuality did you learn in your family? From your cultural group? From the media? From friends or peers? How have these messages had a positive or negative effect on your life and the way you view your body, sex, and sexuality?
2. What were the rules that you were taught about sexual behavior? Make a list of these rules and place a "+" or "−" near each, depending on whether the rule has a positive or negative effect on your life. How do these rules impact your feelings about yourself as a sexual being? Try rewriting the negative ones into positive rules.
3. How has your LGBTQ identity freed you to explore your sexuality and create new, more positive messages and rules about sexuality? What are the positive things you have learned about sexuality and relationships that you think straight people could benefit from?

7

COMPASSION AND EMPATHY

"If I had turned out straight, I doubt I would be the compassionate person I am today."

" . . . the important thing is [a] compassionate heart—then no problem."

The Dalai Lama's wisdom points to the centrality of compassion to our well-being. Indeed, compassion and sympathy are at the root of many of the position themes in this book. Compassion and empathy are at the root of many of the positive themes in this book. For example, when we become aware of our sexual or gender identities, it is through compassion for ourselves that we come to self-acceptance and experience personal growth (see chapter 3). Empathy for others facilitates our close personal relationships (see chapter 4). Compassion and empathy may drive our work for social justice (see chapter 8). In short, compassion and empathy are broad fundamental skills for a positive life.

We often use the word *compassion* when we talk about feeling an emotional connection with others who are suffering.[1] Compassion includes a desire to relieve the suffering of another and may lead us to take action toward that end. The suffering may be minor or major, from vicariously feeling the pain of someone's stubbed toe to being compassionately indignant and protesting unfair and discriminatory treatment of others. Any person who is suffering may benefit from the kind compassion of another. We ourselves gain positive benefits from extending our compassion to others. A 37-year-old "transsexual" from England reflects on how identity inspires compassion (and empathy) for others, "My identity has forced me to think about stereotyping, about being and feeling marginalized, and has increased my empathy with others in minority groups or on the margins. I think I have become a more sensitive, thoughtful, and compassionate person."

Empathy is a similarly broad concept that refers to our ability to recognize and understand the emotions of another person. Empathy may allow us to develop a deeper understanding of another person's inner experience. Whereas compassion focuses on acting with kindness toward someone who is suffering, empathy is more about having an emotional understanding of what the other person is experiencing.

Empathy is a complex skill that requires sensing someone else's positive or negative emotions (for instance, their anger, fear, or joy) *as if* these feelings are our own. When we empathize, we feel an emotional connection to others. A common metaphor is that when we empathize, we put ourselves in someone else's shoes so that we may understand their feelings and experiences more clearly. Empathy may be based on seeing the parallels between our own experiences and the experiences of others, as a 33-year-old "genderqueer" person does: "Experiencing discrimination definitely leads more empathy for others' causes."

Many spiritual philosophies identify compassion and empathy as foundations for peace in the world. Compassion and empathy are based in our recognition of our interdependence and common humanity. Empathy and compassion allow us to share the challenges and celebrate the joys of life with others. Empathic understanding may lead to compassionate actions to relieve the suffering of others. In this way, we experience *self-transcendence*. Self-transcendence, the ability to get outside ourselves and connect to the world around us, can elevate our spirit.

Experiences related to our LGBTQ identities may help us increase our skills of empathy and compassion. We may feel empathy and compassion for others whom we know personally as well as for others we have never met. Empathy and compassion may also extend to animals and all living things.

Some LGBTQ people credit our experience with prejudice as important to the cultivation of empathy and compassion for others who are also oppressed or stigmatized.[2] Our identities as LGBTQ may help us become aware that other parts of our identities are privileged (such as having the status of male, Caucasian, middle class, or able-bodied). Awareness of these privileged statuses may foster compassion for those who have stigmatized identities (such as having the status of female, Latina, poor, or differently abled).

For some of us, experiences of our own gender or sexual identities give us a unique perspective on the experiences of others and broaden our understanding. This perspective may make it easier for us to empathize with or have compassion for others. Compassion and empathy may also prompt LGBTQ people to be more open to others, with a greater respect and appreciation for differences.

SHARED EXPERIENCES WITH PREJUDICE

For a lot of LGBTQ people, compassion and empathy extend beyond those in our own communities to others who are oppressed. Compassion and empathy for others may lead to various types of activism (we also discuss activism in chapter 8). Social justice activism often begins with awareness of the feelings of others who have suffered from prejudice and discrimination and a compassionate desire to do something positive to help. Research findings suggest that when we cultivate our empathic understanding and engage in acts of compassion, we are likely to experience psychological and physical health benefits.[3] Simply put, empathy for others brings about good feelings, as a 36-year-old "MTF straight woman" attests: "Transition taught me empathy and taught me to take a stand for others. I feel good about that and myself for standing up for what I know is right."

Compassion and *empathy* are broad, abstract words. LGBTQ people feel and express their empathy and compassion for others in many ways. For LGBTQ people, empathy can arise from shared experiences of prejudice or discrimination. For some this includes recognition of similarities in experiences of prejudice against LGBTQ persons and prejudice against racial or ethnic minority persons. This awareness may lead to a compassionate desire to confront all prejudices. For example, a 49-year-old in

Rhode Island attributes her understanding of the discrimination faced by other groups to the insights she gained from experiences of discrimination based on her lesbian identity:

> It may seem odd that I consider being a member of a despised, discriminated-against minority group as a positive thing, but I do. It has given me, a white nondisabled woman, some insight into what other groups (such as African Americans, Deaf people, Latinos, etc.) suffer in our society. While my situation isn't the same as theirs, I believe that my not being a fully accepted member of our country's most privileged group (straight, white middle-class people) makes it easier for me to grasp the issues of other disadvantaged minority groups and makes me even more firmly committed to ending all forms of discrimination in our society.

Many others have told us similar stories of feeling empathy for others based on their own experiences with stigma. A "queer lesbian," 34, living in Wisconsin captures this empathic understanding and its impact: "One thing I consider a very positive aspect of being queer/gay/lesbian/trans/bi is that there is a stronger tendency to consider or understand other people's realities and experiences. I think there is a stronger potential to see things from another person's or group's perspective, particularly others who are disenfranchised and discriminated against."

LGBTQ people may have special insight into the experiences of people who have identities that are not fully recognized by others. Positive feelings come from being treated as a whole person, with all of our identities validated. For example, a 36-year-old "Bisexual and/or Queer" woman from Ontario, Canada, shares the empathic consequence of her desire to be recognized for her authentic, whole self:

> I feel that being bi allows me to have a unique perspective compared to gay or straight people. I feel it allows for some level of connection and understanding of other 'in-between' groups such as trans folks, bi-/multiracial people, etc. It especially helps me to feel empathy for people who are in a minority that other people don't see or are a minority within a minority. People often don't see all of me. They label me as gay or straight depending on who I am with. That may be part of me at the moment, but it is not all of me. I feel that allows me to see how other people feel when part of them is made invisible or is not recognized.

As many of the quotes above suggest, empathy and compassion can be important motivators in social justice activism. We have heard many variations on the theme that empathy for people who experience discrimination leads to action. Succinctly put, a 29-year-old gay woman living in Nevada tells how empathy motivates her activism: "I think that being a member of a group that is often discriminated against helps me be empathetic to other stigmatized groups. It also inspires me to 'fight the good fight.' Not just my fight but the fight of others as well."

The skills of empathy and compassion related to LGBTQ identities may be beneficial to developing job-related skills, such as understanding the position of others in need of human services. For example, a 36-year-old lesbian from Tennessee finds these skills are important in her job: "I work in human services, and I think that being a lesbian has helped me to be more effective at my job. I think it has given me the ability to more effectively interact and empathize with clients who, for whatever reason, feel alienated by friends, family, or society as a whole."

Compassionate understanding of others can make us more versatile and accepting in our response to others, allowing us to be more effective in our jobs. A lesbian, 28, living in New York explains the impact of being compassionately open to others:

> One thing that I think is very positive is that I am much more sensitive to others' needs in social situations and responsive to the varieties of types of families that I may encounter in my work, for example—and I pride myself on being able to make other people very comfortable and uninhibited about the 'nonperfect' or minority elements of their own lives. This sensitivity makes me very open-minded about other people's ways of living and their backgrounds: race, religion, culture, mixed culture, family situation, whatever . . .

Experiences with prejudice because of our LGBTQ identities contain the seeds of greater understanding, compassion, and empathy for others. By helping to heal the suffering of those around us, we also heal our own suffering.[4] Thus, our acts of compassion nurture our own spirits as well as those to whom we are reaching out with care and support.

GAY MEN UNDERSTANDING THEIR PRIVILEGE

Some researchers have suggested that having a *privileged* social status (such as *male* or *white*) can interfere with feeling empathy for others who are in distress.[5] We think that these researchers need to recruit some LGBTQ people for their studies—it just might broaden their findings! They may especially want to recruit a few good gay men! We say this because when we asked a large sample of gay men about the positive aspects of their identity, the most common answer we got was their experiences of increased empathy and compassion for others. These gay men place a high value on these insights and skills. That's why we include this separate section about the experiences of gay men, even though the lessons of learning about our privileges apply to all LGBTQ people.

A gay man might initially have a hard time identifying his privilege as male. However, by using his "unprivileged" identity as gay, he may be able to compare and contrast his experiences to learn about privilege, and foster the development of compassion and empathy for others. This experience seems to have a profound effect on many gay men as they become more aware of the experiences of other groups of people who are oppressed. A 37-year-old gay man from Delaware recognizes the lessons of his privilege this way: "I would say the biggest positive for me is the journey from a white male privileged identity to the inclusion of a gay identity which forever changed my experience and passion for working with others who are oppressed."

Many gay men see a direct connection between their sexual identity and their ability to think critically about privilege and feel compassion for others. A 44-year-old man from Maine makes this exact point: "Being on the margins allows the possibility of a keener observation of the human world. I associate my critical thinking ability and compassion for those who are suffering as directly derived from my social status as a gay man." A gay man, 27, living in Kentucky shares a similar perspective on the origins of his empathy for others: "I enjoy being a member of the gay community because it teaches me a lot of things about acceptance, openness, diversity, and sincerity. If I had turned out to be straight, although I would like to think that I would be as accepting of others as I am now, I still would have been missing the perspective that only minority members feel and can share with others."

The experience applies to gay men of color as well as white men. Persons of color may experience stereotyping, prejudice, and a lack of privilege because of their racial or ethnic identity. Nongay (and nontransgender, nonbisexual) men who are persons of color may understand their lack of privilege as persons of color but not fully explore the privileges that they may have as men. However, gay men of color may have extra self-awareness and insight when they explore both their privilege (as men) and their lack of privilege (as men of color and as gay men). For example, a 26-year-old Asian American gay man living in Minnesota speaks of the impact of his identity on his sensitivity to the feelings of others:

> I'm a better person, more sensitive to prejudice and discrimination because I'm gay. I don't think I would have been such an open-minded person if I were not gay. I am a much more spiritually minded person because of the fact that I'm gay. I don't think I would have been as spiritual, had I not been gay. I am better able to understand and make sense of gender identity and human life in general. I am a sensitive, gentle, flexible, loving person because I'm gay. I am better able to relate to others and stand up for others because I'm gay.

A Latino gay man, 34, living in New Jersey describes a similar appreciation for the lessons of his life experiences, which facilitate his compassion and empathy:

> If I were not gay, I don't think I would understand and/or appreciate differences between people (sex, gender, ethnic, race, cultural) as well as I do now. I think sometimes it is really easy for straight men to assume that the world is the way they see it and that people who are 'different' are the ones who don't fit into the grand scheme of things. Being gay has given me an outlook, based on life experience, that we are all different and that we are all somehow on the outside looking in at a very unclearly defined grand scheme of things. I think, also, that being gay has helped me be more sensitive, more human, more authentically spiritual, and more forgiving of others. Absolutely my experiences as a gay man have made me more politically progressive and made me understand power and people in a much deeper way than I would have if I had been straight.

White gay men may take advantage of their privilege as white men to address other white men about oppression. Speaking as a peer and as an ally of oppressed groups can be influential in changing prejudiced attitudes. A 25-year-old gay man from South Carolina tells this story:

> I think that my experience as a member of an oppressed group also helps me to empathize with other members of oppressed groups and to more readily see the subtle forms of oppression that exist in society. I can also help to speak about this oppression to typically resistant groups (heterosexual white men), because until I tell them that I am not like them, they assume that I am like them. That is another positive aspect of being gay and out. The strength and courage one develops from repeatedly coming out tends to bleed over into many other areas, including confronting prejudice in all forms.

When we have a privileged status, we have an opportunity to use both our privilege and our experience of not having privilege to cultivate wisdom. Fenton Johnson, in his book *Keeping Faith: A Skeptic's Journey Among Christian and Buddhist Monks*, eloquently writes, "The poor and oppressed do not have to labor for the gift of understanding that the world does not 'belong' to them; that is the nature of their reality. To the extent that being gay has given me access to that wisdom, I am blessed."[6]

Like Fenton Johnson, many gay men have come to realize how their power based on one identity (as male) and their oppression based on another identity (as gay) influences their relationships with others. Importantly, LGBTQ people can translate their growing self-knowledge about their privilege into positive feelings and actions. We might call these "conscious acts of compassion."[7] Learning about our privileged statuses and then using that social power to benefit others is an act of compassion that transforms our own lives and the lives of others.

A UNIQUE PERSPECTIVE

Life experiences with our LGBTQ identities give us multiple perspectives from which to view the world. As a "trans, queer" 29-year-old from Illinois notes, "Being trans has helped me understand and empathize with other people's struggles in a way I could not otherwise. It makes me think about my world in a way that I could never do otherwise." Indeed, we may form a *unique perspective* based on an accumulation of experiences related to our LGBTQ identities.[8] For example, this may happen through experiences of being treated differently depending on the type of relationship we are perceived to be in (for example, a same-sex versus a straight relationship, or perhaps a monogamous versus a polyamorous relationship). Or we may experience life from the perspective of more than one sex or gender.

These unique perspectives, based on our experiences, foster our understanding and ability to have compassion and empathy for others. For example, some transgender-identified people have been treated at different times as a man *and* a woman. These experiences combine to create a unique perspective leading to a greater empathy and compassion for both men and women. An "MTF straight woman," 43, living in Ohio relates to the experiences of men and women: "It has been a very positive lesson for me to see the world from the position of being treated like a man, pressured to be very macho, and now as a woman, being pressured to act submissive. I have an insider's view of both experiences and have empathy for how confining both roles are."

For some transgender individuals, experiences with hormonal changes increase the level of understanding and empathy for both men and women. For a 25-year-old "Lesbiman Queer Texan," the transition process allows this valuable insight: "I have had the experience of going through puberty two times, once as a female and once as a male. This gives me more empathy for members of both sexes. PMS is terrible for women. I am one of the few men in the world who really understands what they go through. Also, I understand menopause because I've technically gone through that as well."

A "Gay FTM Queer," 47, living in Michigan echoes this understanding: "I have the unique ability to understand what it is like to be female identified and male identified. When a woman talks about personal medical issues (e.g., PMS), I have a good understanding of what she is talking about. At the same time, I know what it feels like to be male, though I was not socialized as a male."

Another type of unique perspective comes from having different types of relationship experiences. For some LGBTQ people, these experiences may result in empathy for others in a variety of relationship types. For example, a 47-year-old "bisexual queer" woman from

Wisconsin understands the challenges of different types of relationships and identities:

> I do think my life experiences with long-term partners of different sexes have given me a unique perspective on the world and an ability to relate to a wide variety of people. I can listen to and relate to the relationship challenges other people are having regardless of what kind of relationship they are in. I also think my being a visible bisexual breaks the tendency of many queer communities to privilege gay/lesbian over bisexual, transsexual, gender queer, and intersexed.

Having a unique perspective based on our experiences may broaden our views and extend our compassion and empathy. This ultimately benefits our own well-being as well as the well-being of the community.

OPEN TO THE EXPERIENCES OF OTHERS

Appreciating people who are different from us transforms our views and increases our compassion and empathy. When we appreciate diverse experiences, we realize that ours is not the "only way" or the "right way." Parker Palmer, a sociologist and educator, notes that being open to others who are different takes courage.[9] Having courage and challenging the status quo can be a positive aspect of LGBTQ identities. For example, identifying as queer may result in being more open to others, more open to challenging the status quo, and more open to creating a new, more respectful approach to life and relationships. A 27-year-old queer woman living in California suggests this broad impact: "I think the concept of queerness has the potential to teach the world new ways of being good to one another, respectful, open, communicative, daring, and unconventional."

LGBTQ individuals often experience being "the other" in social relationships.[10] We may experience being treated as less than equal and as different (from the conventional). Being treated differently can help LGBTQ people develop an appreciation of how differences between people create opportunities for learning and growth. Being open to these opportunities is a positive experience for many LGBTQ people. For example, the lessons we gain from recognizing when we are treated differently may lead to compassion for others who are treated differently. A 32-year-old "Bisexual Queer" from the state of Washington expresses this openness and appreciation:

> One of the greatest assets to being bisexual in my experience is it provides me with compassion and understanding for the 'gray' areas of life. I feel I am more open to variety, difference, fluidity, and 'otherness' from my own experiences in these areas and from being misunderstood by various communities, including the queer community. I have felt a strong alliance with the trans community, as so many individuals within that community have expressed similar struggles with fluidity and otherness and being misunderstood, which I see as an asset to helping bridge the different communities within the queer community.

Several people have expressed to us that their bisexual identity gives them a special appreciation for others. They perceive themselves as generally less judgmental and more open and empathic toward others because of their identity. A 29-year-old bisexual man from the United Kingdom finds his openness to be a positive value: "The last thing we need is to become sexuality-centric in how we approach others. Avoiding such attitudes takes effort, but the trials of bisexuality have equipped me well in this respect. So to conclude with the most positive aspect of my bisexual identity, I would say that what I value most highly is my compassion, tolerance, and broad-mindedness toward others."

Compassion assumes fundamental equality between people and involves feeling a deep respect for others.[11] Using the lessons of our identities may yield a greater respect for others and increased ability to see our common humanity. A "bi, half gay" woman, age 21, living in New York sums it up nicely: "I think the most positive thing about being bisexual, for me, is the ability to accept people for who they are. It doesn't matter what you look like, if you're a man or woman, where you come from, or what you do, we're all the same deep down. Despite language barriers and oceans, we all have the same basic needs: to be loved, cared for, helped, comforted, and understood."

Many of the world's social problems may be related in some way to a collective lack of compassion. Yet as individual human beings, we each have the ability to be compassionate. Our basic human nature is to seek happiness through our positive connections to others. The empathy that results from exploring our experiences in relation to the experiences of others may result in a broad and inclusive commitment to social justice. A 30-year-old gay man from Texas explains how his identity informs his recognition of the many prejudices that need to be challenged:

> Being gay has engendered in me a commitment to social justice. Being oppressed, I actively work to confront and overthrow oppression in all its forms. Because of my experience as a gay man, I have a heightened level of empathy that translates into my desire to challenge racism, sexism, classism, ableism, sizeism, etc. Being gay allows me to be less constrained to the limits that are placed on other men and has helped to buttress my altruistic impulses.

For LGBTQ people, cultivating compassion in our own lives and working to promote more compassionate social institutions and communities are important contributions to the well-being of ourselves and society.

MY EYES OPENED: A 60-YEAR-OLD WHITE, SOUTHERN, GAY MAN FROM VIRGINIA

> Being gay has given me experiences of discrimination that have opened my eyes to the plight of other people and individuals. I think being gay has made me more empathic and compassionate than I would otherwise have been as a white, Southern man. White, male, middle class, well educated. I was born into all these "privileged" states. I can think of no other status that has made me oppressed—save one, my identity as a gay man. This single factor opened me up to oppression and gave me the opportunity to become increasingly aware of others' oppressions and to empathize. This is one of the single greatest gifts of being gay. In no way can we or should we compare oppressions, but I am thankful for the opportunity to have my eyes opened to a part of the human experience that I might not have seen otherwise. I would have missed so many fulfilling experiences if I had not had my eyes opened.

EXERCISES AND ACTIVITIES FOR REFLECTION AND PRACTICE

Exercise 1: Becoming Empathic and Compassionate

The following questions ask you to reflect on how your LGBTQ identity has shaped your capacity to empathize with others and show compassion. These questions are food for thought, and you may want to record your answers in your journal.

1. How has your LGBTQ identity helped you understand and empathize with other persons who are stigmatized or are targets of prejudice?
2. Can you think of a specific instance when your LGBTQ identity contributed to your ability to empathize and have compassion for another person or group of people? Can you think of ways you may show your compassion and empathy in the future?

Exercise 2: Practicing Empathy and Compassion

Meditation has been demonstrated to increase empathy and compassion for self and others, enhance relationships with others, and even improve physical health.[12] The following daily practice is derived from exercises suggested by His Holiness the 14th Dalai Lama as a way to increase compassion.[13] Try it for the next four weeks and notice the effects on your sense of well-being and on your relationships.

At the beginning of each day, spend five minutes remembering that all human beings want to be happy and loved and that we are all connected to one another. You may want to think of a friend and how you are connected. Then think of a stranger, maybe someone you see on your way to work or in your neighborhood. Think of how that person also wants to be happy and loved. Think about how you are connected to that person.

For the next five minutes, first, while breathing in, feel compassion for yourself. Then, while breathing out, feel compassion for others. If people come to your mind that you have difficulty feeling compassion for, try to understand their life experiences and extend your compassion to them.

As you go about the activities of your daily life, extend an attitude of kindness and compassion to everyone that you meet. Practice kindness toward the least powerful and the most powerful people you encounter. Extend kindness toward those you love and also to those you may feel dislike toward. See if your dislike becomes less intense when you try feeling compassion for them.

8

MENTORS, ROLE MODELS, AND ACTIVISTS

"I want to go beyond myself and make a difference."

"Until the great mass of the people shall be filled with the sense of responsibility for each other's welfare, social justice can never be attained." Helen Keller reportedly made this observation, and we think it is an appropriate sentiment. Our "sense of responsibility," and the actions that we take to fulfill our responsibility, can contribute positively to our sense of well-being. Pursuing positive goals may enhance our self-esteem and give us a sense of purpose and meaning in our life.[1]

LGBTQ people can find many ways to fulfill a sense of responsibility for the welfare of others. We may act on an individual level, interacting one-on-one to mentor others. We may be role models for a few people, or many. In sharing our LGBTQ identities, we may be activists just by being visible. Or our activism may take place in a larger arena, pursuing equality for LGBTQ people or social justice on local, state, national, and international issues.

Mentoring is an active process of guiding and nurturing the personal growth and development of someone else. The person we mentor is typically younger or has less experience than we do. Mentoring contributes to our own well-being, to the development of the person we are mentoring, and to the health of our communities.

Role models are important to us as we grow and develop, even in adulthood. We tend to find our role models at school, in our communities, at work, and among our family and friends. Sometimes we find them on television or through the virtual world of the Internet. Finding role models who share our sexual or gender identity can be more challenging because of the lack of access to a range of visible LGBTQ persons.[2] Certainly, we need leaders, mentors, and role models who exemplify how to lead fulfilling lives and help us develop positive LGBTQ identities.[3]

At some point, however, we may realize that not only are we looking for role models, but we ourselves have become role models for others! We may be a role model as an individual or our relationship may be a model for others. Being a positive role model is very satisfying. It is a responsibility and one that LGBTQ people can take on wittingly or unwittingly. When we become aware of it, the positive feelings that come from influencing others and helping them (by giving them something we often wish we had) is rewarding. A gay man from New Jersey, 53, acknowledges the contributions of being a positive example for others: "A positive aspect of being gay is being part of a larger struggle for equality. We are making progress in this struggle, and it is nice being part of the movement leading to this change. I feel that the way I live my life—openly, affirmatively—helps improve things for those who come after me. I want to be a positive example of actively working for change."

Activism is a very broad term. For example, educating people around us about food insecurity around the world and what we can do to help is a form of activism; going to another country to teach sustainable agriculture or starting a local community garden are different forms of activism on the same issue. Activism in the pursuit of social justice, whether by being a role model for one person or joining a mass demonstration for equality, is a positive activity that enhances our sense of well-being.[4]

When we say *social justice*, we are talking about the fair distribution of goods and benefits in a society (and yes, we could probably argue all day about what is "fair," but in the end we would most likely find that we agree on more points than we disagree). For many LGBTQ folks, social justice activism is an important extension of their empathy and compassion for others (see chapter 7). It may include LGBTQ rights as well as other broad social issues (although we believe all social justice issues ultimately affect LGBTQ people and are therefore LGBTQ issues). For example, we may contribute to making the world a better place for all people by working on broad social issues such as environmental preservation and restoration, ending poverty, protecting reproductive freedom, religious freedom, animal rights, and civil rights for all persons.

Actively working toward social justice helps to provide a sense of meaning and purpose in life. It is an expression of our values, which is important to our feelings of well-being. Activism is a future-oriented activity—working to make the world a better place. When we engage in social activism, we express our optimism and hope for the future. Activism also typically involves being part of a group, which heightens positive feelings associated with belonging and making a contribution. LGBTQ activism benefits us in all of these ways.

MENTORING AND BEING A ROLE MODEL

Although being a mentor and a role model often overlap, mentoring is a specific type of activity. Mentoring is part of an interpersonal relationship. It involves trust between two people. A mentor teaches another person knowledge and life skills through personal interaction. A mentoring relationship may be formal, as it often is in work or educational settings, or it may be informal, as it often is in our friendships or social networks.

Mentors can be any age, but often we become mentors as we grow and learn—that is, as we gain the knowledge and wisdom that comes with age and experience. By the time we reach the middle part of our adulthood, we may develop a specific interest in helping others learn new knowledge and skills. This may be part of giving back to our community. This developmental stage is sometimes called *generativity*.[5]

Perhaps one of the biggest needs in the community is mentoring for LGBTQ adolescents and young adults as they come out and transition into their adult lives. Young LGBTQ people need positive mentors (and role models) who will inspire and encourage them to live authentically and flourish. A 33-year-old "bisexual queer" woman from Wisconsin recognizes her responsibility and influence in a community of young people: "Being able to be a role model/mentor for LGBTQ youth and modeling positive identity for both LGBTQ youth and straight youth is very positive. It is a great way to be an activist."

For many LGBTQ people, acting as a mentor is a way of providing something to someone else that we wish we had had at an earlier point in our lives. For example, a lesbian, 34, living in Florida mentors a young woman who is newly out. Providing this young woman with the mentoring relationship she wishes she had had when coming out is a very positive experience:

> I became a mentor of sorts to a young woman who was the daughter of a close friend. It made me so happy to know that she felt she could come to me for support, and I always took time to be with her when she asked. Because I had gone through some of the same experiences, I felt like I could help her. I would have loved to be able to talk to someone that I could trust when I was her age. I feel lucky to be able to be there for her.

A particularly important role for mentors is helping others sort through the social pressures that they experience. Mentors can help another person find their authentic expression and their own core values.[6] A 35-year-old "trans-woman, bisexual" views her mentoring of others as "payback" to those who had mentored her:

> I find being a mentor to others the most rewarding aspect of going through the transition experience. It's a way to 'pay back' those who helped me and taught me so much when I was struggling with my identity and how to find who I am. And it's a way to 'pay it forward' to those who come later. We have to rely on each other to a large extent for knowledge and wisdom (trust me, they don't teach you anything about being transgender or transsexual in school!). We have to support each other and help the new generations by being there for them like our elders were there for us. I'm a mentor and a role model for anyone who needs me.

A role model is someone that we would like to emulate or model our own behavior after. Role models can inspire us. They show us what is possible through their actions. A role model may show us how to cope with challenges and turn them into opportunities for growth. Hearing other LGBTQ people's coming-out stories, for instance, can inspire us in our own coming out and model for us how to live authentically.

Being a role model may be a private activity that occurs within our own families and local communities. Many LGBTQ people are role models through their parenting or grandparenting or by being an involved aunt, uncle, or sibling.[7] Some LGBTQ individuals are role models for other people's children through their service as a teacher, coach, or community leader. In many instances, we might not even realize we are a role model to someone else unless they tell us. For one 35-year-old gay man, the opportunity to be a positive role model is part of what inspired him to become a physician:

> I would say that being an African American gay man increases my capacity to relate to other people. Especially other people who are misunderstood, and I think that does help me be more empathic and compassionate for other folks. Because a lot of times until you experience something, you can't relate. And because I've been through it, people understand that I can relate. In regards to being African American and gay, I've learned that it's hard. But I think I'm a pretty good guy. And so if I could go out and help other people realize that they're good people too, being black or gay or both, then that's what I'm called to do. And I will admit, I've done a lot of stuff on purpose. I know that people are more prone to listen to doctors. And people are more prone to listen if you are nonviolent in your protest. People are more prone to listen if you try to establish a connection with them. And so I, being where I am as an accepting gay man and a successful African American man, I owe it to other black/gay men to make it part of my calling and part of my purpose to give back to them. To be a visible role model or mentor or whatever it takes.

In our own youth, we look at the people around us, adults as well as peers, for models of how to act, dress, express ourselves, and what to think (among other things). Because the lives of LGBTQ people have historically been less visible, it can be difficult for LGBTQ youth to see visible role models in their immediate surroundings. (This is also true for us as LGBTQ adults.) Some may find LGBTQ teachers or education professionals as role models. Others may find role models in the workplace. A gay man, 35, from Virginia, for example, realizes that he serves as a role model at work: "I find it positive to be a role model for the gay community in my workplace. I enjoy being openly gay in the workplace, particularly where I work with younger gay and lesbian students (interns) who look to me for support and guidance."

Our influence as role models is not limited to other LGBTQ people. LGBTQ individuals also model character strengths and important values for those who are non-LGBTQ. For example, a "genderqueer FTM," 28, living in Texas tells about educating and inspiring others:

> I get told over and over, by trans-identified people and non-trans-identified people, that I am an inspiration to others. People thank me for having the courage to express and say who I am. They thank me for teaching and/or sharing with them a new perspective. For being brave, bold, or daring. Non-trans people have even gone so far as to thank me for helping 'to make the world a better place' or 'usher in a new era.' These kind of flowery but sincere speeches sometimes confuse me a little, but I think the gist of what most of those people are saying is that they feel that my gender identity (and my expression of it) helps to create a safer and more harmonious world for all. This might seem a little overblown, but this kind of response to my coming out as trans has actually become kind of a common experience for me. I have also been told that I am a leader and thanked for that. I know I have inspired other FTMs to come out as trans or FTM or genderqueer, because several have told me so. It is positive to be an inspiration or influence to others. Other non-FTM-identified people have told me that I inspired them to feel safe to explore their own gender and/or sexual identities.

Opportunities to be a role model and educate others may come as part one's work life. Volunteer activities may also provide these opportunities. A 22-year-old "bisexual lover of women and men" from California talks about her interactions as a volunteer with young women in an after-school program:

> I get to educate others about the myths of bisexuality and to deconstruct the negativity surrounding this label. For example, in my high school girl group they always asked and questioned my sexual identity. They would always ask me if I was a lesbian. I said no. I am out to them now, but I was always surprised when they never followed up with asking if I was bi or even if I just liked women. Also, a few of the girls used homophobic language, such as saying 'no homo' and calling people 'gay' and using that term in a negative way. So my coming out to them was very important because I wanted to be an educator about bisexuality and LGBT issues, in general. They looked up to me, so I thought it was important to be honest

with them. Even before I came out, I was always the one to place LGBT questions and things in games, activities, and lesson plans for group. It's very important for high school students to be aware of LGBT issues and to not discriminate against someone based on their sexual identity or gender expression/identity. It is also important because some of them will grow up to be LGBT.

THE MODEL COUPLE (MODELING RELATIONSHIPS)

Most LGBTQ people want to find a partner with whom we can share our lives. As we discussed in chapters 5 and 6, many LGBTQ individuals feel free to *"make up new rules"* and new roles in their intimate relationships. But that doesn't necessarily mean that we want to create everything from scratch. Many of the same-sex couples that we have interviewed over the years tell us that they want positive role models for their relationship.[8] One 34-year-old gay man from Kentucky expresses this desire to find relationship role models at the same time that he and his partner are serving as role models for their friends:

> My partner and I would love to meet other gay couples who have been together for a long time, like twenty or thirty years. I think it would be great for our relationship to be able to talk to couples who have been through what we are going through and talk to them about what they did. It's weird sometimes, we've been together for seven years and already some of our friends think of us as 'long-term' and are asking us questions.

Same-sex couples share a lot of similarities with heterosexual couples. For example, satisfaction in intimate relationships is linked to physical affection, equality between the partners, and a lack of major conflict for all types of couples.[9] While happy and satisfying couple relationships share these similar qualities, same-sex couples face some unique challenges.[10] On the positive side, some research studies have found that many same-sex couples could teach heterosexual couples a thing or two about how to divide household tasks equally, manage finances fairly, and deal with conflicts in ways that are constructive and not destructive to the relationship.[11]

Communication is an important component of a satisfying intimate relationship. For LGBTQ couples, being willing to communicate is an important part of showing commitment in a relationship.[12] A 61-year-old lesbian from Ohio explains how she and her partner of thirty years model relationship communication for their kids:

> I know it's a stereotype, but we [my wife and I] process about everything in our relationship. We made an agreement early on to never avoid talking about something important. Our kids watched this growing up and now their spouses tease them about wanting to 'process like lesbians.' But they also thank us for showing them and teaching them how to talk about things. One of our son-in-laws told us what great role models we are for their relationship. He said that sometimes they get stuck in an argument and say, 'What would your moms do?' They try to think about how we might talk about tough things. That's probably the biggest compliment we could ever get from our family.

It is important for LGBTQ couples to see positive, long-term, committed, loving relationships around them. For this reason, it can be a source of satisfaction for LGBTQ couples to be role models for others. A 40-year-old "bisexual lesbian" from the state of Washington writes about her family and friends' view of her twelve-year relationship: "They see that we are happy together, complement each other, are good forces in each others' lives, and they admire our relationship." A gay man, 38, living in Pennsylvania told us a similar story about being a relationship role model for younger LGBTQ people: "Younger people look up to me and see you can be gay, happy, and in a committed relationship. My partner and I have been together for eleven years now. We're not just old boring guys; we have a lot of fun. Younger people see that and see that the stereotypes about gay men not being able to commit to a relationship are just a bunch of bull."

Being a supportive friend to other people and couples (LGBTQ and non-LGBTQ) may enhance a couple's relationship. Some LGBTQ couples receive less support from their families of origin than their heterosexual married siblings do. These couples tend to rely more on their friends and chosen family for support for their relationship.[13] By being a role model for others, they may return the favor. A 46-year-old lesbian living in Texas, who has been with her partner for twenty-one years, finds giving support to other couples to be an important positive aspect of her identity and relationship:

> I think the most positive aspect of being a Lesbian has to do with providing support for Lesbian friends that may not receive the same family and community support that I am fortunate enough to receive. I think my partner and I, working as 'out' lesbians, try to set an example and be good role models for ALL our friends, including our lesbian friends and couples. It brings out the best in us and we feel a responsibility to other lesbian and gay couples to share our good fortune and be supportive of their relationships.

ACTIVISTS FOR LGBTQ RIGHTS

Public figures, whether celebrities or just people in visible positions, can be role models for people they know as well as for people they have never met. Many of us perceive ourselves to be activists simply by virtue of being out and being authentic. Perhaps that is part of the reason that the feminist saying "the personal is political" resonates with many LGBTQ people. This is true for a lesbian, 42, living in California: "I like belonging to an alternative group of the population and feeling like I am a part of a political and cultural movement that is very important in our world today. I like the fight for human rights and continuing work toward equality. Being a lesbian is making the personal political, being politically active just by being out."

Actively Educating

LGBTQ identities can be invisible or unrecognized. This lack of visibility may lead to opportunities to educate others, sometimes by actively *becoming visible* and dispelling stereotypes as a form of activism. A 36-year-old lesbian from Colorado finds her initial invisibility to be an opportunity to actively construct her visibility and educate others: "I am aware of social justice and civil rights issues in everyday life. I'm aware of my status as an 'invisible' minority. I work for civil rights issues. I tend to look at myself and my life as an opportunity to educate others about not assuming too much and living my life as an example of what stereotypes I am not." A 38-year-old "queer bisexual" from Idaho also identifies the educational opportunity associated with initial invisibility: "Given that people assume I am straight unless I say otherwise, it allows for some invisibility. While the invisibility itself is not always positive, it does allow me to build relationships with people who may not initially realize that I am queer identified, and as a result, our positive relationship helps to change their mind about LGBT issues."

Being visible in addition to being authentic is an important part of individual activism for many LGBTQ people. For example, a bisexual woman, 22, living in Indiana challenges other people's assumptions about bisexuals in an effort to educate them:

> I like that I've led some friends to question their own stereotypes or prejudices. I'm a relatively quiet person and don't really fit how a lot of people imagine bisexuals to be, and I think speaking about my sexuality with some people has forced them to change their perceptions of bisexuals (or sexual minorities in general). I've had some people apologize to me for just assuming I was straight until I told them otherwise, and I think they might remember that and carry that with them when they start to make assumptions about others' sexual orientations. It sounds pretty lofty, but I think speaking candidly about my bisexuality is a way of challenging heteronormativity, even if it's only within my group of friends.

Sometimes educating others is a more intentional form of LGBTQ activism. Educating others about the group or groups we identify with may hold special import. For instance, a "Gay Transman," 27, from Pennsylvania educates people about both of his identities: "It is important to me to be an advocate and educate audiences about misconceptions and stereotypes. It is even better when I am able to educate them through my own experience as a transgender individual and my identity as a gay man." A "bisexual, queer" man, 33, from Canada intentionally discloses his identity to prompt questions and create the opportunity to educate others: "I feel privileged to be able to answer questions about bisexuality in a frank and earnest way by being an out individual—hopefully thereby spreading positive information about bisexuality in place of fear and bias."

Educating others may extend to a broad range of issues beyond our own identity. Influencing the opinions of straight people on a variety of

LGBTQ issues is an important goal for a "Bi-girl," 23, from Louisiana: "I think that being bi has made it easier to talk to my peers about things that affect the queer community as a whole. I am very vocal about marriage rights and various other issues, like issues that transgender people face or immigration issues and asylum issues. I feel like I can make a difference by getting other (straight) people to support us."

Political Activism

LGBTQ people may be involved in a wide variety of political activities. There are interpersonal activities like having conversations to persuade others to support a candidate or a public policy issue. For example, we might talk to a neighbor about voting for marriage equality and against marriage restriction amendments in state constitutional ballot referendums. Or we might wear a campaign button, have a bumper sticker on our car, or put up a sign in our yard showing our support for a candidate. Contributing money to campaigns or organizations is another type of political activism. Writing letters to the newspaper, blogging online, communicating with our elected representatives, lobbying, or going to a march or rally are all common forms of political activism. Positive political involvement increases our sense of well-being by giving us a way to express our values through our actions.[14] A 57-year-old "trans-woman" from Florida experiences these rewards in being politically active: "I have found it to be a positive thing to be active in fighting for civil rights for GLBT persons. To be able to work for those protections is very rewarding. We need to encourage everyone to get involved."

Numerous organizations pursue LGBTQ equality at the local, state, national, and international levels. Some organizations focus specifically on LGBTQ rights (such as the National Center for Lesbian Rights or the National Gay and Lesbian Task Force) and others have a broader social justice agenda (such as the American Civil Liberties Union or Amnesty International). Political activism may take place at many levels. For example, a 37-year-old gay man from Illinois supports LGBTQ rights at several levels: "I come to the defense of gay rights during discussions with family, friends, and coworkers (and occasionally people I don't know). I have joined a national gay rights organization and a local gay rights organization. I participate in political outreach. I do a lot of online activism. I speak up for myself and I speak up for others."

By participating in political activities, we may experience empowerment, or the sense that we have some personal influence in political events and can achieve important goals.[15] Feeling a part of a larger social movement is valued by a lesbian from Nebraska, 27: "Being gay has given me things to fight for. There are things that are simply not right in this world, such as the lack of equality of GLBT people. Being active in the political scene lets me feel like I am part of a movement—something that will change society forever."

Participating in social activism can lead to a meaningful connection to the larger LGBTQ community (we talk more about this topic in chapter 9) as well as our local community. For example, in a 2009 study, youth who were active in a gay-straight alliance (GSA) reported feeling connected to a larger community, lessening their feelings of isolation. As leaders in a GSA, youth activists felt empowered to help education and mentor their peers as they work together for social justice in their schools. They also reported that participating gives them a voice and teaches them how to use their knowledge and skills in ways that make a difference for others at their school.[16]

Adults also find a sense of belonging and support from participating in organized efforts to promote LGBTQ rights. A 41-year-old gay man from Utah explains the connection he feels as a result of being politically active:

> Being a gay man in America in the latter half of the twentieth century has been an amazing experience. I feel VERY fortunate to have been alive during this time period in part because of the emergence of the GLBT community as a recognized group. I have been active through the years in a number of activist groups, political organizations, and demonstrations, including marches on Washington and protests. This type of connection to a larger GLBT community has been very important to me.

SOCIAL JUSTICE FOR ALL

Many LGBTQ people are active in fighting for issues that address social justice more broadly. As we noted in chapter 7, many LGBTQ people express empathy and compassion for other oppressed or minority groups. Taking on the role of ally, then, becomes a motivation for our activism. For example, a gay man, 52, from New Hampshire elaborates on how his identity led to his awareness and activism as a feminist:

> I have been an active feminist as I realize that fighting the limitations of gender roles does much to create discussion of and freedom for LGBT people and same-sex relationships. We have to see and treat everyone, women and men, as equals. We can't put women in certain roles and then devalue them. That devalues everyone. I have experienced being devalued as a gay man, especially when someone thinks I am doing something 'feminine'—like helping my mother clean her house. A couple of my uncles have told me that 'that's women's work' and I shouldn't be doing it. But I know my mother doesn't have much money, in part because she was discriminated against in the workplace because she did 'women's work' as a secretary (for a guy who made a lot of money and couldn't have done it without her being organized and taking care of things, but he paid her very little and gave her no credit). When I see all of this, I can see the vicious cycle of discrimination and I want to change things so that my sisters and my lesbian friends are paid equal and get equal credit. And if we value women and what women do equally, then when men do the same work or are in a relationship and clean their house, it's all seen as valuable. So we all have to actively work for women and men to be equal, in government, at work, and in society.

Having social interest, or living beyond ourselves and working for the common good and betterment of society, is an important part of our humanity. We need to encourage and cultivate, in ourselves and others, social or community interest.[17] The awareness of one type of oppression can lead to fighting many types of oppression. A 27-year-old lesbian from Texas explains this domino effect of social activism: "Because of my awareness of oppression (as a lesbian and as a Latina) I've become involved in social justice organizations attempting to eliminate white supremacist and patriarchal ideals as well as homophobia." A 27-year-old gay man from North Carolina similarly comments on his broadened agenda for social activism: "Because I am a gay man, I am more concerned with social justice, not only for LGBT issues, but any minority, the disabled, children, and so on."

At midlife, many LGBTQ people find new meanings in their lives.[18] These new meanings may come from the lessons we learn in facing adversities. How we face those challenges, in turn, makes us more aware of the adversity faced by others and what it might take to meet those challenges.[19] That awareness may translate into a stronger commitment to social justice for all human beings. Our commitment to social justice activism can become part of our life legacy.

Social justice activism may also help LGBTQ people to enhance our leadership skills.[20] We know that LGBTQ-identified individuals have been effective leaders in many social justice organizations, either in front of or behind the scenes. Putting our leadership skills to good use is rewarding and enhances positive well-being. Anytime we engage in purposeful action that adds meaning to our lives, we enhance our well-being. A gay man, 40, from Alabama embraces his opportunities to lead: "As I get older, I become more active as a person, more involved in the community and the issues that affect me on a small level and a greater level because I am gay. I realize that my voice counts. I can't sit on the sidelines. I need to get out front and lead in this fight."

LGBTQ people have been leaders in numerous organizations working for social justice. Whatever the form of activism, the sense that we are *doing something* is important. The desire to fight for civil rights is a strong positive motivator for many. A 43-year-old "Transman, just a man" from Tennessee sums it up: "I think it is very positive that I do not allow ignorance to influence my life, I do not follow Internet-generated trends or believe rumors, I do not allow discrimination for any reason . . . either grandma raised me right or by being an intelligent Transsexual I learned to fight for right instead of just being a victim." We suspect it is a lot of both. (Thanks, grandma!)

A MENTOR AND A ROLE MODEL: 55-YEAR-OLD LESBIAN FROM ARIZONA

I think being a role model is positive. I work in a big office and have contact with a lot of younger people just starting their careers. I find it especially gratifying when the young gay men and lesbians (and several 'questioning' ones) come to me and can talk openly and ask questions about being out at work and how to handle certain situations with coworkers. I think it makes them feel like they have an ally and someone they can look to for advice. And I think some of the questioning ones just watch me to see how I handle myself, and that makes them feel more comfortable with their feelings. I think my partner and I are also role models because we have been together for twenty-eight years—longer than any other couple in my family. Our younger brothers and sisters, and even our nieces and nephews, have told us that they want to have a relationship just like ours. I think they really look to us, not the straight people in our family, as the model for what a relationship should look like—equal partners who love each other, support each other, and talk about things.

EXERCISES AND ACTIVITIES FOR REFLECTION AND PRACTICE

The following questions and activities are designed to help you think about the role models and mentors that you have and the ones you may want to find! Or you may take on the role of mentor to someone else. You may want to participate in different types of social activism. Use the following questions to evaluate the role of activism in your life and make decisions about your own contributions to making the world a better place.

Exercise 1: Write a Gratitude Letter to One of Your Role Models

Who are the people that you have looked to for inspiration about how to live a meaningful life? Write a letter to someone who has been a role model or who has inspired you in some way. If possible, hand deliver your letter to this person. This gratitude letter exercise has been shown to have positive effects on the well-being of the grateful person (and no doubt also has positive effects on the person who is the recipient of the letter!).[21]

Exercise 2: What Would My Role Model Do?[22]

Are you facing a particular challenge in your life right now? Some people have found that it is helpful to carry a picture of their role model with them as a source of encouragement. As you go through the process of solving a problem, or working through a challenge, or even if you just need a concrete reminder to maintain your optimism and hope, you might draw on what you have learned from your role model. Then answer the question, "What would [insert role model's name] do?"

Exercise 3: Being a Role Model

Do you think you are or have ever been a role model for someone else? Has anyone ever told you that you are a role model for them? What did they say?

Most of us vastly underestimate our impact on those around us. What types of positive messages do you want people around you to receive from the things you say? What small actions can you take to be a positive role model of life well-lived as a person with an LGBTQ identity?

Think about people who are younger or less experienced than you are (in a job, at school, or some other setting) that you spend time around. How might you be a positive role model for these people? How can you reach out to affirm and encourage the goodness and potential of others? Who do you personally know that needs a positive LGBTQ-identity role model in their life?

Exercise 4: Engaging in Social Activism

How would you like to improve your community? Make a list of three to five concrete things you would like to see happen.

What concerns for social justice do you have? Make a list of three to five big concerns that you have.

How have you worked or might you work for social change in your community? Is there an important issue that you would be willing to give time and energy? Sit down and list three to five organizations or groups that you might join, contribute money to, or get involved with in order to pursue the changes you want to see happen.

Think about ways you might urge others to work for social justice. How can you approach and talk to them? Make a list of three to five people (for example, family, friends, or peers) that you want to talk to about these issues and about getting involved.

Exercise 5: Self-Care for Social Activists and Role Models[23]

Social activism is often a long-term project that requires stamina. Social change does not happen overnight. So to remain effective and avoid burnout, it is essential that social activists learn to balance their social change efforts with personal time to refuel, replenish, and renew. Here is a starter list of self-care activities for the social activist. Add your own personally meaningful activities and make specific plans for regular self-care.

1. Take care of your body. Engage in regular physical activity through recreational activities, sports, or an exercise program. Eat healthy foods.
2. Nourish your spirit. Create your own relaxation ritual. Some people meditate; others listen to relaxing or inspiring music, take a hot bath or work on an art project. Or you may want to read books, watch films, and enjoy artistic creations that uplift and inspire you.
3. Nourish your relationships to self and others. Spend time cultivating friendships with people who nourish you emotionally; spend some quality time alone each day to plan, reflect, relax, or check in with your feelings (you might want to write in your journal).
4. Mine the moment. Tune in to the small satisfactions and pleasures of the moment. Get in the habit of looking around for something or someone to appreciate. Notice and savor your awareness, even for just a few seconds.
5. Five-minutes-to-joy technique. On an index card, write a positive "slogan" or quote or mantra that helps you refocus, relax, or regroup. Tape it to your computer, your mirror or refrigerator, wherever you can see it throughout the day. Examples of these slogans include "I'm learning and growing" or "all is well" or "let it be." Some people use a question to help them focus on their priorities and values, such as "What positive thing can I do right now?" or "What is my intention right now?" The important thing is that your slogan or question be positive and personally meaningful.

9

BELONGING TO AN
LGBTQ COMMUNITY

It's a great community to be a part of.

Got *Pride?* Where do we search for role models for our LGBTQ identities? How do we become LGBTQ activists? Where do we find our
friends and family of choice? Where do we go to feel safe, supported,
and like we belong? For many of us, the answer is the LGBTQ community.[1] Or LGBTQQIA! (This includes questioning, intersex, and allied
individuals as part of our community. If we've forgotten to include a
letter, please forgive us. We want to be all-inclusive!)

The term *community* has many meanings. A community often forms
around shared interests or experiences. Community can be a large,
extended informal social network of people that we know. Community
may be virtual, a web community, or a social network, such as an online
support group or a fan page for a group. Community activities can take
place in a physical space where people gather to socialize. Sometimes
community forms around shared activities such as reading or traveling.
Our community may include acquaintances or even strangers that share
our identities or support us.

Our community may include structured organizations, such as schools
we attend, our workplace, or religious groups. A sense of belonging
within these groups facilitates our feelings of well-being. Teenagers, for

instance, spend a majority of their time at school and in school-related activities. They perform at their best when they have a sense of belonging to their school community.[2] The same is true for adults in their workplace. What is important is that our communities provide the opportunity for connection and participation.

The LGBTQ community includes groups of people that come together, physically or virtually, because of their shared sexual or gender identities. These groups may be social, political, recreational, formal, or informal. They may provide support or be based on common interests or identities.[3] Belonging to an LGBTQ community may benefit people in many ways.

It is fitting that this is the last theme presented in this book because being a part of the LGBTQ community is related to many of the positive aspects of LGBTQ identities we have covered in the previous chapters. Community is a place to be ourselves and explore new roles and ways of expressing ourselves. We have compassion and empathy for others who have similar experiences to ours and welcome them into our community. We may look to our communities for social connection and to find our intimate partners. We can find role models and be role models in the community and work with others for social justice.[4]

For most of us, finding community means finding support for coming out and a safe space to express our LGBTQ identities. The LGBTQ community also provides opportunities to create networks (social, professional, or both). For example, a gay man living in Florida finds advantage in the fact that *"we are everywhere"*: "Being an out gay man creates instant networks. When moving, I can always join the GLB chorus and have an instant social group. Some places I can just walk down the street to a coffee shop where gay people hang out and find instant community."

LGBTQ people may experience the LGBTQ community as a *collection* of communities. Some people may connect more with just one part of the larger community. For instance, a lesbian may feel most comfortable at lesbian cultural events or a transgender person may feel more at home and supported in transgender or queer spaces. On the other hand, many LGBTQ people find strength and cause for celebration in the diversity of the larger LGBTQ community. A 29-year-old gay man from Massachusetts explains how big the community is in his mind: "The word gay encompasses a lot when it comes to our community. I mean, lesbians, gay men, and to me it includes bisexuals and transgender people. Everybody can fall under that umbrella in a sense. And so, that's part of the reason why I use the term gay. I try to take some pride in us all being together." The sense of being part of one big community, with common experiences that bring us all together, is an important positive connection.

SUPPORT AND SOCIAL NETWORKS

Belonging is a fundamental human need. Humans are social beings and need to have a sense of belonging or connection to others.[5] Our sense of belonging is often based on some commonality. The commonality may be as simple as living close to someone (our neighborhood community) or being in the same workplace. Or it may be based on shared identity, interests, or experiences.

In finding or building a community around ourselves, we meet important needs in our lives. In community, we find support. The LGBTQ community may support us in our coming-out process and provide an ongoing sense of belonging and connection. It may also provide a safe space to be authentic, to be ourselves, and to express our identity. We may intentionally look for other LGBTQ people to befriend or network with, especially in new places, because that helps us to feel safe, like we belong, no matter where we are.

Support for Coming Out

Coming out may include unique personal and interpersonal challenges and is often an ongoing process. We often look for support during this process. Reaching out to the LGBTQ community can be an important connection for many. Although there is considerable diversity within the LGBTQ community, we may also find similarities of experience that serve as a basis for community building and social support. The LGBTQ community offers many resources, including groups based on mutual interests and passions (for example, chorus groups, softball or bowling leagues, or businesspersons' networking groups) and groups based on life experiences (for example, coming out, parenting, or transitioning). Finding these groups may help us integrate our LGBTQ identities with other aspects of our lives. They may help us create a space where we can express our whole self.

For most people, their family of origin provides support through many of life's developmental stages and transitions because their family members have already been through similar experiences. However, LGBTQ people may need to look elsewhere to find someone who has had the experience of, for example, coming out or transitioning. A 23-year-old transgender person from California discusses the importance of community in addition to family: "It's nice to have a supportive community of those who know what it is you are going through. My family has been okay, but they just don't understand how I feel. These people, the trans community, get it and can help me."

Feeling accepted by a community empowers us to embrace our identities as LGBTQ people and address the challenges that we face. A gay man, 35, living in Illinois makes the point, "When I first came out, it was the discovery of a community (friends, boyfriends, social scene, politics) that really was empowering. It made me feel not alone in what I was going through." Since most of us do not have immediate family members who share our LGBTQ identities, finding this kind of community support during the coming-out process (and beyond) can be invaluable (see also the discussion about chosen families in chapter 5).

We can return the favor by supporting others in the community. The act of giving back to the community connects us to others and enhances our sense of belonging and being effectual. A 46-year-old British, "bi, queer" man enjoys organizing community events to support others:

> I've discovered an amazing subculture of people who also identify as bi and [I] now feel part of a community for the first time in my life. I get a buzz out of supporting other people who are just making the first tentative steps toward a bi identity. I've become very involved in organizing bi-related events. This is my way of paying back all those who I met and who supported me during my early days of finding my identity.

A Safe Space

The LGBTQ community may represent a safe space for many people in physical as well as psychological or emotional terms. Where LGBTQ identities are still stigmatized or not supported, providing this safe space is an especially important function of community. Having a stigmatized identity can lead to negative experiences with prejudice. Even though this is a book about the positive aspects of LGBTQ identities, we also need to acknowledge that there are places that do not feel safe to us. Hate crimes, harassment, and discrimination against LGBTQ people are unfortunate realities. Contrary to what is often said, LGBTQ people are not necessarily *invisible*. When we live honest, authentic lives, we are often quite *visible*. In some places, being visible as LGBTQ can make safety a primary concern, especially for those of us who bend or break the rigid gender rules.

For these reasons, it is important to have safe spaces for ourselves and to create safe spaces for others. Feeling like we are part of the LGBTQ community may include a feeling of being in a safe space. Our community may provide a feeling that there is safety in numbers. Or a sense that anyone who is in a particular space must be there because they are supportive of us. The LGBTQ community can offer this sense of safety, support, and stress relief. A lesbian from Nevada, 28, captures this good feeling in her story:

> The good part of being a lesbian is that when I'm somewhere in the GLBT community, I feel I can be open about my sexual orientation in a positive, supportive environment. I feel an almost overwhelming sense of liberation. The oppression, discrimination, and stigmatization that comes with being something other than straight creates an immediate bond with others who are not straight. While we may have all had different experiences, there's still a common bond. We've all played the pronoun game (changing she to he), had some kind of coming-out process, gone through the stages of realization and acceptance of who we are, etc. Knowing that there's someone who can relate to that aspect of your life means a lot. When we are together, we can let our guard down and relax for a while without feeling like we might be judged.

Finding ways to connect with the LGBTQ community may include attending parties, marches, coffeehouses, or rodeos, or joining a softball or rugby league (to name just a few of the many places we can find other LGBTQ people). These types of community gatherings offer times and places to bond with others, feel safe, and renew our positive energy.

This renewal has positive effects on our physical and mental health. A 25-year-old "bisexual trans-woman" has found in community a place to feel safe and supported: "Finding a supportive community has been the most positive thing in my life. I can't begin to tell you how positive it has been to find places to be myself, to not look over my shoulder, to just enjoy life. These people, trans and gay and bisexual, just let me be me. They give me a place to breathe freely."

Networking

Community may be a small group of people, including our close friends and allies. Or we may be talking about a big community of acquaintances, friends of friends, and even strangers in a new city. There are many resources, including books and websites, that serve to help LGBTQ people find each other. Even when we travel to a new place, we can often connect with other LGBTQ people. A 31-year-old gay man from Texas connects through the common bond of "shared experiences" with other LGBTQ people: "There is a community of support for me anywhere I go simply because I am gay. There is a level of bond between LGBT people due to their shared experiences (e.g., coming out, being discriminated against, etc.). I can make a connection with a total stranger."

Recognition and acknowledgment of other LGBTQ people leads to a variety of connections. For some it is an informal, in-passing nod of the head as we walk by someone. That nod may be very meaningful in making us feel like we are part of a community. A 30-year-old gay man from Kentucky explains this "camaraderie" very eloquently:

> I want to say instant camaraderie is the most positive thing about being a gay man. It's not that all gay people agree on everything, but there's a common thread that every gay person has to accept in themselves and then they have to also kind of accept their role in the larger society. I could never truly claim my gayness until I came out to myself and then could go out and truly connect with someone else. And in a sense, it is similar to the 'black factor' for me because as a black man, even to this day, I'm walking down the hall at work and I see another black man and we lock eyes and we nod our head and there's an instant respect and instant camaraderie, even though he doesn't know me from anybody else and I don't know him from anybody else. But we know that we share a common experience. Maybe we are mis-

guided in thinking that. I mean, there are a lot of assumptions in that head nod. He assumes that I've been probably persecuted because of race and I assume the same for him, and that makes us feel more connected to each other. I would say it is the same when I pass a gay person. We nod to each other. It makes me feel like I'm part of something larger. So I'd say that the positivity of being gay for me is just instant acceptance in a community.

LGBTQ identities may enhance opportunities for networking in the workplace. For example, being in a broad social network helps us meet people in a variety of professions. These connections may come in handy in our jobs, in running a business, or if we need services. A 26-year-old "gay-trans" person living in Connecticut recognizes the business advantages of networking in the LGBTQ community:

> Gay identity provides a great sense of community. I have a number of excellent networking opportunities at work and socially. I get to meet a lot of people, and you never know who you will need to call for some business need. I have a bunch of business cards from gay people I have met at parties that I go to first to see if I can find someone in the community to give my business to.

There are many formal and informal professional groups for LGBTQ people. Some workplaces (companies and institutions) sponsor LGBTQ (and allies) employee affinity groups. Research has demonstrated this to be a smart business practice. These groups provide a sense of belonging in the workplace and increase employee loyalty. The groups also provide a means for LGBTQ employees to ask for inclusive business or organization policies and practices.[6]

In a workplace, LGBTQ groups bring together employees from different parts of an organization. They come together to share their experiences and concerns. They also end up creating a network for communication across the hierarchies of a business. This is beneficial to the business as well as the individual. A gay man, 37, from North Carolina elaborates on his experiences with this type of networking and the benefits for him and his company:

> Where I work, I have noticed that I have a broader network than most of my coworkers. I tend to know the lesbian vice president and the gay male janitor rather than just sticking to my peers like heterosexuals will

often do (studies have shown that people of color and smokers do this too, although I don't recommend taking up smoking!). I learn a lot about the company this way. Bottom line, I think it helps me be a better manager than my peers because I am less isolated.

FIVE DIFFERENT COMMUNITIES TO CHOOSE FROM

The LGBTQ community has been described as being five separate communities under one big mashed-up label. Each may have its own distinct cultural features. Its own lingo. Its own space. If you look at some of the travel guides for LGBTQ people, they often note whether a bar has, for example, a primarily gay male clientele or has a "lesbian night." Some bars have multiple floors where one floor is known as "trans-friendly" and another floor is "mixed." In short, there are differences between the communities, and some of us seek out a specific community within the larger LGBTQ community.

At some points in our lives we may feel the need to immerse ourselves in groups of people that we perceive to be most like ourselves. This may serve to help us strengthen our sense of identity. At these times, we may seek connections to a group of people who most closely share our identity and our experiences. Activist Robyn Ochs notes, "There is a time for coalition-building, and a time to get together in our own identity groups to do our own empowerment work." (p. 246).[7] A 33-year-old "transgender, genderqueer" from Georgia agrees:

> One positive aspect about being transgender and genderqueer is my relationship to the trans and queer community. I feel like my gender and sexuality have a home in a unique culture where I can freely express myself. Having trans and queer space means I always have a place where I can get and lend support and can have access to activities and events geared toward the community. Whereas in mainstream culture my identity would be marginalized, in trans and queer spaces, it is celebrated and normalized. In addition, I think the trans and queer communities are more progressive in general than our straight counterparts. As someone with progressive politics, I have found that I can expect most of my trans and queer friends and acquaintances to be on the same page regarding other social issues (like being antiwar, pro-choice, antiracist, etc.). I think

that being part of a minority community means that these folks are more open to considering other progressive issues.

Many lesbians talk specifically about the support of the women's community. *Women's community* is a broad term. For some, it may be code for a primarily lesbian community or women-only spaces. At its broadest and most inclusive, the term refers to all women (or at least the subset that is supportive of other women or who identify as feminist). A 28-year-old lesbian from Ohio notes the support she feels from the broader women's community: "As a lesbian, I can fundamentally connect with the experiences of women. This guides my art and my activism. Other women can relate to that. I am always supported by the larger women's community in my artistic, activist, and academic endeavors."

Other lesbians specifically talk about their connection to the lesbian community. A 46-year-old lesbian living in Vermont is clear about where she finds support and feels connection: "Lesbian communities offer both the social connection and a kind of intangible sense of power/empowerment in being a part of a large group of very capable, independent, and creative women." Finding this sense of empowerment in any community is positive for our sense of well-being.

The lesbian community supports a culture that includes a set of events, lesbian entertainers, authors, and celebrities. A 44-year-old lesbian living in Arizona points out the community-building function of lesbian culture: "The best part of being a lesbian is the lesbian community, the lesbian sensibility. This community will talk about anything; nothing is off-limits, nothing is sacred, at least not for long. I love the lesbian comics. They are making jokes about lesbians, but they are really pointing out how much we have in common and share as a community." For a lesbian, 29, living in Washington, D.C., lesbian culture provides a place to meet other lesbians: "I love that if I want to be surrounded by lesbians, I can just find out what lesbian musician is playing, or what lesbian author is having a reading, or what lesbian play is at the theater. Lesbians are very loyal, and I can go to any of these and see people I know."

The word *gay* is often used as a shorthand way to refer to an inclusive LGBTQ community. Let's face it, one syllable is much easier to say than five tongue-twisting letters or listing out every group (that's twelve syllables!). Because *gay* is often used inclusively, it is sometimes unclear whether or not gay men are referring exclusively to a gay male community when they talk about their connection to a *gay* community.[8] Other times the exclusive connection *is* clear. For example, a gay man, 38, living in New York is specific about his ties to the gay male community: "The best part of being a gay man is getting to hang out with a bunch of wonderful gay men. Whether it is the gay men I bowl with or the Bear Pride meetings I go to, I feel like I am part of a gay community."

Some bisexual-identified people talk about feeling more at ease in the bisexual community. A 35-year-old "bi, queer, femme" living in Ontario, Canada, enjoys her ties to the bisexual community: "I love bisexual culture. My bisexual community, my close circle of bisexual friends, have really made my life rich and fulfilling." For others, the bisexual community, sometimes in contrast to the gay/lesbian and heterosexual communities, is perceived as being more welcoming to people of all sexual orientations. This inclusive feeling creates a space where a bisexual identity is supported along with other sexual or gender identities. A 49-year-old "bisexual queer dyke" appreciates this openness to all of her identities: "I have found that the bi community is an open-minded and supportive space to be yourself. No matter if you are with a man, a woman, a transperson, or more than one partner, the bi community is very accepting of personal choice, and I love that. I have found the bi community to be very supportive personally and politically of transpeople, and that is important to me as well."

Subgroups of the larger LGBTQ community are important to finding social support and understanding. These subgroups may be particularly important for LGBTQ people who also have an ethnic or racial minority identity. The need for separate groups that form around different multiple identities highlights the diversity that exists within the LGBTQ community. In addition to these smaller groups, many find that a larger group that is inclusive of multiple identities is empowering.[9]

FINDING STRENGTH IN A DIVERSE COMMUNITY

We've heard some people say that the LGBTQ community is really five separate communities thrown together once a year for a Pride parade. You might agree with this view after reading the section above. For some people, at least some of the time, having a separate community is important. At other times, uniting as an inclusive community of lesbian, gay, bisexual, transgender, and queer-identified people is a source of positive energy and strength. This is illustrated by the comment of a young lesbian from Wisconsin: "A positive thing about being a lesbian is the sense of community among GLBT people. Despite our differences, we are all in this together and need to support each other."

The LGBTQ community has a culture that, at its best, imparts a sense of positive identity and belonging. Culture includes customs (ways of acting and communicating), traditions and rituals (regular occurrences like Pride festivals), histories (connections to the past), and symbols (such as the rainbow flag). These cultural histories, symbols, and activities help to anchor our sense of identity and belonging. A stronger self-identity leads to a stronger sense of well-being.

A 23-year-old "gay lesbian" living in Ohio recognizes the positive aspects of this cultural richness and connection to her identity:

As a Caucasian person growing up in our society, I was always jealous of the cultures that were cherished and nourished by people of other ethnicities. I felt like I didn't belong to any particular cohesive group in which I could take pride. When I finally admitted to myself that I was gay, after struggling with it for many years and knowing it was true my whole life, I finally realized that I am part of a minority group and a culture full of pride. We make our own families. We have our own lexicon, our own bars and restaurants. For me, knowing that I belong to a rich and colorful community is the most important positive aspect about being a lesbian.

Within the LGBTQ community there is enormous diversity. There are LGBTQ people from all racial and ethnic groups and geographic locations, including all other nations. There are people from all religious and spiritual backgrounds. People of all ages, abilities, and income levels. People from every job category. Diversity is a strength of the community and presents a positive opportunity to learn about others that differ from ourselves. In short, we may share the same gender or sexual identity label, but we come from everywhere in all shapes, colors, sizes, and abilities. Each of us makes a unique contribution to the community.

Recognizing and celebrating the incredible diversity of the community is important. The ability to appreciate the complexity of the human beings that make up our community enriches our lives. This is true for a lesbian, 32, living in Nevada: "I find the gay community (men and women) to be an incredibly diverse tribe . . . you can draw strength and positive energy from it and utilize those tools to improve yourself and build a better and more understanding society." A 41-year-old "bisexual, queer" man from Berkshire, England, agrees: "I like the diversity in the GLBT community. Socializing with other GLBT people, many of whom are out about being 'different' in other ways (vegetarian, vegan, polyamorous, science fiction geeks, environmentalists, and so on), I get to experience a lot more diversity than I do socializing among people who identify as being straight."

The LGTBQ community is a place for sharing experiences and interests and building alliances. For example, when gay men and lesbians work to be strong allies for people who identify as transgender or bisexual, and vice versa, the community becomes stronger. Being allies enriches our lives. No longer are we just working for social justice in the abstract. We are actively forming relationships that celebrate our differences as we learn about each other and share our time and resources. One important way to contribute to community is to help create a welcoming space for all LGBTQ people, a space that is free of the prejudices of racism, sexism, ageism, ableism, and classism as well as homophobia, biphobia, and transphobia.[10]

A lesbian living in California, 38, explains her commitment to being an ally of all groups in this way:

> On a community and political level, being a lesbian (and a feminist) has helped to further politicize/radicalize me and given me the opportunity to be a part of a diverse LGBT community, which invigorates me and strengthens my resolve to fight for equality and to encourage others (in and outside of the community) to embrace diversity and the principles of feminism and social justice in general. I think being a lesbian (and a feminist) has helped me to be further committed to social justice for all groups and to be a proud and vocal supporter of all oppressed peoples. Given my own experiences as a lesbian and a woman in general living in a patriarchal and homophobic society, I also feel I am a better ally to those who are penalized in the areas for which I am privileged (my racial and class status). As a white, upper-middle-class lesbian, I understand the notion of intersecting oppressions and the fact that most of us experience

privilege and penalty simultaneously. As a lesbian feminist, I feel obligated to both fight inequality and acknowledge the various ways in which I am privileged, and to struggle to end systems of privilege/penalty. On a professional level, I am gratified to be able to contribute to social justice and to combat heterosexism and homophobia as an out lesbian at work.

When we join together as a group, there is political power in numbers. The LGBTQ community has an interest in creating policies that affirm our citizenship and include all of us fully in society, without discrimination.[11] The community is where we can work for these changes in concert with others. For example, the community may host a debate for political candidates to put pressure on politicians to vote for inclusive nondiscrimination policies (covering sexual orientation and gender identity) or to support equal relationship recognition for all couples. Forming a *voting bloc* (people who are likely to vote together for the same candidate) is a statement of community will and power.

Working together for civil rights and social justice has been at the heart of LGBTQ community throughout its modern history (we discuss this more in chapter 8).[12] A 39-year-old gay man from Rhode Island believes this strength in numbers and unity makes an impact: "Being a part of a larger GLBT community has a positive impact on our local, state, and national politics. The community has consistently supported progress. They can't totally ignore us when we band together."

ONE BIG FAMILY: 50-YEAR-OLD "LESBIAN, QUEER, DYKE" LIVING IN ILLINOIS

It was the March on Washington in 1993 that taught me how diverse the LGBTQ community is. I had been out for a long time. I had worked for over a decade for gay rights. I had been to several parades and marches before. But there was something about that March on Washington that made me appreciate the LGBTQ community as just that—one big community. Just to see all of those people there, first of all, was amazing. The U.S. Park Service said there were like 300,000 people there. Anyone who was there knew that was a lie, but you could never get the federal government to admit that there were a million queers together in one place demanding equal rights. That would just be too scary for them. And then, to see all the different people: Asian, Black, Latino, Native Americans (indigenous persons), and White people, young and old, men and women and drag queens and punks and business suits and men and women in leather . . . the list just goes on and on. [By the way, I am not denying that there were certain groups that were under-represented at the March. I am just recognizing the amazing diversity of LGBTQ people.] Even a lot of straight people and their kids (although I think a few of them were visitors and thought they would have a quiet day visiting the Washington Monument!). It was just a feeling of one big family. I don't like crowds at all. In fact, I am rather claustrophobic if I get in a crowd, so I get anxious and look for the quickest way out. But I felt a surprising calm and peace at being surrounded by this group of queer people who were smiling and happy, but were there with a pur-pose. That is community. It still makes me smile to think about it and the power of it and I'm glad I am part of it.

EXERCISES AND ACTIVITIES FOR REFLECTION AND PRACTICE

Finding support in the LGBTQ community is important to a positive view of ourselves. The following questions will help you think about your connections to the LGBTQ community and how you might in-crease your sense of community.

Exercise 1: Reflecting on Your Community

Consider the following questions. You might want to record your answers in your journal.

1. How would you describe your sense of the LGBTQ community or communities?
2. How has the LGBTQ community had a positive impact in your life?
3. Are you satisfied with your sense of connection to the LGBTQ community? If not, what steps might you take to become more connected to the community and thus gain and provide the kinds of support that enhance life satisfaction?

Exercise 2: Increasing Your Community Connections

Actively contributing to your community can increase well-being. This activity may help you to find new ways to contribute your time, talents, or other resources to your community.

1. Make a list of your interests and passions.
2. Find out what LGBTQ groups are organized around your interests, either locally or on the web.
3. Pick one group or activity to try this month. Go to a meeting, take part in an online discussion, or engage in some way with this group.

Exercise 3: Picture Your Community

In order to *visualize* our community connections, it can be helpful and fun to literally sketch them out or visually illustrate them. The following exercise is adapted from Ivey, Ivey, and Zalaquett (2010).

Use your own unique artistic style to illustrate your community. You may want to use a piece of poster board or large piece of paper with colored pencils, markers, or paints. Or draw on your computer tablet. Use whatever medium suits you.

Start by representing yourself with a significant symbol or picture. Place yourself at the center of the drawing or at another appropriate spot.

Think about the most influential groups of people or organizations that make up your personal community. Place these groups on the drawing and map out your connections to illustrate their importance to you or their influence in your life.

Once you have represented these parts of your community, think about the strengths of your community. What positive stories come to mind? These positive aspects of your community can be important resources in your life.

A POSITIVE VIEW

This is a very positive part of who I am.

Be *all that you can be!* Thrive! Flourish! Embracing and cultivating positive LGBTQ identities can help us live well. It's time to start a new conversation; a conversation that focuses on the positive stories in our lives. These positive narratives can help us meet life's challenges, grow through all of our experiences, and enhance our sense of well-being.

As researchers, we have interacted with literally thousands of people who identify as lesbian, gay, bisexual, transgender, and queer—and a lot of variations on these themes! What we find is that LGBTQ people seek to live their lives with a sense of fulfillment and satisfaction. These are basic human goals. What we also find, and try to convey in this book, is that our LGBTQ identities can have a positive impact on our lives and help us pursue and attain these goals.

The eight affirming themes that we talk about in this book are broad and cover a lot of ground. You may have additional themes from your own life experience that you could add to this list. That's great! This book is just a starting point for exploring a positive view of LGBTQ identities.

We believe that the themes we talk about in this book are accessible to everyone. For example, if we feel that it is difficult to openly share our LGBTQ identity with other people (like some of the experiences of people quoted in this book), reflecting on that experience may help us develop more compassion for others who have difficulty expressing or sharing their identity or experiences. Increasing our compassion for others makes it more likely that we will experience a deeper sense of purpose or meaning in life. In this way, cultivating the positive lessons of our LGBTQ identities makes our life more positive and fulfilling.

Historically, professions like psychology, social work, and medicine (as well as many other academic disciplines) have focused on problems, deficits, and illness rather than strengths, assets, and wellness. In other words, there is a tendency to look for things that are "wrong" and to try to "fix" those things. Addressing issues that have a negative impact on our well-being, such as depression, anxiety, and alcohol or drug abuse, is extremely important. However, in focusing solely on what's wrong, we can sometimes forget to appreciate and support what is positive and "right" in our lives.

We want to reframe the conversation and focus on a positive view of LGBTQ identities. We want people to recognize that embracing and cultivating positive identities can help in addressing the issues and challenges we face in life. This in turn enhances our overall sense of well-being and helps to create the conditions in our lives where we can flourish.

In this final chapter, we add a couple of "bonus features" to our eight themes. The LGBTQ people we have interacted with during our research have impressed us with two additional positive qualities. First, the sense of humor that comes through in many of the answers to our questions is entertaining and, we recognize, is an important part of LGBTQ well-being. Second, the sense of optimism, stated explicitly and implicitly, is a notable feature supporting LGBTQ well-being. We discuss each of these bonus features in more detail below.

We then discuss the impact that multiple identities and diverse cultures may have on how LGBTQ people experience or express their sexual and gender identities. These cultural identities or backgrounds may limit or change the individual expression of some of the positive themes discussed in this book. Or they may add new variations to these themes.

Finally, we challenge ourselves and others who have the privilege of claiming LGBTQ identities to use our positive strengths to make contributions to social justice for everyone.

A QUEER SENSE OF HUMOR

One thing that has made our work easier and more pleasurable to conduct is the sense of humor that many LGBTQ people convey in their interactions with us. As we said in the introduction to this book, studying minority stress (as we sometimes do) is stressful in itself. We can often see and hear the impact that this chronic stress has on people's lives. Some of the stories we have heard over the years can only be described as tragic or heartbreaking. But many times, looking back, LGBTQ people are able to find some humor even in the darkness (while still recognizing and not minimizing the harms). Humor can be part of a positive coping strategy for dealing with stress. Some people perceive that their sense of humor is greatly influenced by their LGBTQ identities.

For a lot of LGBTQ people, their identities come with a side order of a sense of humor. Whether it is of necessity or just an artifact of looking at the world *"through gay eyes,"* humor is an important feature of LGBTQ lives. In our original research survey, a sense of humor was rarely mentioned in specific terms as a positive aspect of LGBTQ identities. However, many people clearly displayed their sense of humor as they told us their stories. So it's more like a thread that weaves through our interactions than a theme per se. Although a few people did specifically name having a sense of humor as a positive aspect of their LGBTQ identities. For example, one gay man, 44, observed, "Being gay sharpens my sense of irony. I can see the absurdities in life and laugh, when other people are just bewildered or clueless."

A sense of humor is a common coping mechanism for dealing with challenging situations. The old adage "If I didn't laugh, I'd cry" suggests that humor can be a positive way to cope with an otherwise painful situation. Using humor to highlight the absurdity of prejudice or discrimination can help us feel better or maybe safer in a less-than-welcoming environment. Humor may disarm someone who is trying to put us down. It may point out the ridiculousness of someone's prejudice. It may help us keep a healthier perspective on a situation rather than internalizing negative messages and feeling badly about ourselves. And certainly when we tell the story later, it can be a lot funnier than when it actually happened.

Humor has its place in our identity expression and can help us feel more positive about ourselves. A 26-year-old "gay man-lovin' Oklahomoan" explains the role of humor during his coming out:

> Coming out, I mean, it's been hard. But the one thing that got me through was this sense of humor about it all. You have to be able to laugh at yourself just in general. If you ever take yourself too seriously, I'm sure that leads to more stress hormones, which leads to more depression and other bad things. But I think it shows a level of acceptance once you can laugh at yourself. Because you know, nobody is perfect. I have lots of physical attributes that I'm not very proud of, but I laugh about them and I move on. And I think that same thing with being gay. There are lots of things about being gay that are difficult, but if I can laugh about them, especially laughing with friends, I think that's important. I think that a sense of humor, especially in the gay population, helps not only to bring us together, but it also helps diffuse attacks from the outside. So I'd say that learning to laugh is my biggest gift from being gay.

Humor may help dissolve tensions in our interactions with others. We have heard several stories about the function of humor in tense situations similar to this one from a 28-year-old "queer drag queen":

> If you are queer in this world, you have to have a sense of humor. When someone is looking at you like they might hurt you, sometimes it's all you got. Being a drag queen has taught me to appreciate the humor in things and have a quick wit. My friends appreciate that too. I might have been kinda funny if I weren't a 6'2" drag queen, but I know I'm a lot funnier the way I am. It's a feel-good part of my life.

A sense of humor about our own identity (and identity group) is helpful when we are confronted with stereotypes and their ridiculousness. Even though people around us may be well-meaning, they may have been exposed to negative stereotypes and feel some discomfort in communicating with LGBTQ people. A gay woman from Florida tells how she uses humor in an attempt to alleviate the discomfort of well-meaning others:

> You have to be smart about it, but having a sense of humor, including about being gay, can help to put everyone at ease. Some people are basi-

cally good at heart but don't know what to say around gay people. If I tell a little self-deprecating joke, they relax. There is humor in our stereotypes, and we can use that to make a joke and let other people see that humor. They usually get the idea that a stereotype is wrong more quickly by making a joke about it than by sermonizing about it.

Some of the LGBTQ community's most well-known public performances are drag shows. If you've never been, don't be afraid—just go and see for yourself. We are pretty sure you will end up laughing. Among other things, these performances often serve as a humorous expression of the excesses in rigid gender roles and rules. As a 33-year-old "genderqueer" living in Georgia notes, "I appreciate the way LGBTQ plays with gender. We put on so many performances (drag, burlesque, etc.) that are not only entertaining, but are also gender transgressive. I really appreciate our ability to use humor and fun in breaking down stereotypes about gender rigidity."

Queer humor may come from having a different perspective. It may also come from having a unique, insider view of LGBTQ culture. A 30-something Pennsylvania lesbian uses her insider view to create a long list of positive things about her identity, having fun with many stereotypes about lesbians and lesbian culture in the process:

> Once upon a time, I was asked why I thought I was gay. I said, 'I don't know. I just always figured I was born lucky.' That's pretty much how I feel about being a lesbian. For me, there are so many positive aspects that it's hard to make an exhaustive list. So here's a partial one . . . 1) I get to sleep with women. 2) No one ever expects me to show up in a dress. 3) People think I have innate knowledge about mechanical things. 4) No one ever asks me to put their stuff in my purse. 5) No one would blink an eye if I had 100 cats. 6) I can hang out in cool gay nightclubs without feeling like an interloper. 7) My being gay actually scares some people, and I sort of like knowing that I could rob a mini-mart armed with nothing more than my projectile homosexuality. 8) It's perfectly fine for me to own ten pairs of Doc Martens. 9) I am culturally obligated to remain best friends with all of my ex-lovers. 10) I get to participate in the bacchanalian frenzy that is the Pride Parade. 11) If I identified as a lesbian who likes to chew on rocks, there would be a support group for that. 12) Oh, and did I mention . . . I get to sleep with women.

Having a sense of humor has beneficial effects on our health and sense of well-being. Humor that is kind and promotes social cohesion (relating to a common experience) is hopeful, life-affirming, and satisfying (so, please, be kind in your comedy!). Humor can be self effacing or sympathetic. It can help promote compassion for others or motivate people to take action.[1] In short, laughing and smiling will help us feel more positive about life.

A SENSE OF OPTIMISM

In our opinion, people in the LGBTQ community are, generally speaking, an optimistic bunch of folks. We have sometimes been surprised by how much hope LGBTQ people express, even in the face of prejudice and discrimination. For example, in our study of the passage of state constitutional amendments restricting marriage equality, we found optimism and hope to be major positive coping strategies for LGBTQ people.[2] Optimism, or having good feelings about the future, is important to our sense of well-being. We believe that optimism underlies several of the themes in this book. For example, optimism may inspire us to social justice activism.

Optimism is looking forward with the belief that good things will happen or things will turn out favorably. Seeing the world and life as positive is important to living a satisfying life and having a sense of well-being.[3] Optimistic people who face challenges and adversity can look forward, realistically, with hope and a belief that things will turn out well.

While optimism may not be a direct result of LGBTQ identities (or it could have something to do with it), it certainly can help LGBTQ people to have positive experiences with our identities. For example, optimism may be expressed in the coming-out process. While many people may initially be hesitant or fearful about coming out, optimism may help LGBTQ people feel that everything will turn out okay. For example, a 24-year-old "queerly gay" college student from Maine expresses the optimistic change in his life after coming out:

One positive thing is that I've learned to be more positive about my life in general. I'm more positive about the future since I came out to my family and friends. I used to think negative things a lot. I always expected the worst. Now I feel that since I can be honest about myself that good things will happen. Even if everything is not good all the time, it's not the end of the world. I just go on being me and it will look up.

For some LGBTQ people, optimistic feelings fuel our activism. Social justice activism is about believing that we can make the world a better place. It is about visualizing a better world and working toward that vision. Some people simply label themselves as optimists. Others explain the process of optimism inherent in their actions. For example, an "Asian, bi, genderqueer," 42, from Oregon speaks explicitly of his optimistic motivations:

> I have to be optimistic about the future. That is what keeps me going. It comes from being a minority in multiple ways. I can't just make the world better for one of my identities. It has to get better for all people so that it is better for all of me. Then my bi identity, my queer identity, my Asian identity—none of that will matter. We'll all just be humans—with special features!

Optimism plays a special role in creating positive identity. The sense that things will get better, will turn out okay, and that we will find happiness is a great motivator. A 71-year-old gay man exemplifies this:

> I still get up every day and ask myself 'how can I make the world a better place today?' I think it's because I'm gay that I don't take things for granted. I still worry about the future and want to make a difference. I have six grandchildren and two great-grandchildren. I want the world to be better for them. I want it to be better for the young gay kids (including my grandchild who is gay). Some people seem to think that everything is okay for gay kids today. That it's so much easier than it used to be. I want that to be true, but we still have work to do to get there. I want it to be true in my lifetime and I think it can be if we all work to make things better. It may sound funny, but being gay has made me be more optimistic so that I can keep working toward the goal—a better world.

MANY CULTURES AND MULTIPLE IDENTITIES

We know from various sources that there are people throughout history, in all geographic locations and cultures, who have experienced sexual attractions or intimate relationships with persons of the same sex or whose gender identity is not simply male or female, or whose sex is not the same as the appearance of their bodies. We also know that *lesbian*, *gay*, *bisexual*, *transgender*, and *queer* are relatively new words in the vocabulary of the world. These labels may not even translate in some languages.

We acknowledge that social context may place limitations on how the positive themes in this book are experienced by people from different racial, ethnic, or cultural backgrounds. As we discuss briefly in this book, the LGBTQ labels are not claimed by everyone. Further, they might not even meaningfully exist in some places. Or these words may be seen as "Western" or "American" words. The Internet and other mass communication technologies import and export identity labels to many corners of the world, but certainly not all.

In many cultures there may be limits on how the themes in this book are experienced or expressed. In cultures where there are no words for same-sex sexual feelings, it may be difficult for a person to even know what they are feeling. Or strong prohibitions against expressing any variation in a gender identity may mean that even acknowledging one's inner experience is not possible at present. Recognizing these limitations, we do not suggest that the themes in this book are a "one-size-fits-all" way to look at LGBTQ identities.[4] There are many ways to understand sexual and gender identities and express them in positive and affirming ways.

Research supports the idea that having a strong ethnic or racial identity and a strong sexual or gender identity can be complementary and part of an overall positive identity experience for LGBTQ people. For example, we know that feelings of belonging and having strong social networks within their communities that support both parts of their identity are especially important to the psychological well-being of Latina lesbians and Latino gay men, African American lesbians, and African American gay and bisexual men.[5] It is quite likely these findings about the benefits of social support for our multiple identities apply broadly to LGBTQ people from all racial, ethnic, and cultural backgrounds.

Many fascinating books, articles, websites, and movies present information about sexual and gender identities in other countries and cultures. Some of these are historical and others are current.[6] Some are about cultures within the United States and others are about cultures elsewhere in the world.[7] We encourage our readers to enjoy exploring these resources to better understand the context and diversity of LGBTQ identities (and other sexual and gender identities).

We do suggest that several of the positive themes presented in this book, in their general form, are universal, or nearly so, to the human experience.[8] Wanting positive connections with others is part of being human. Empathy and compassion are human emotions. Growing and learning is part of living as human beings in the world. These positive themes apply to everyone regardless of our identities, where we live or what culture we grow up in.

FINAL THOUGHTS

We want to express a final word of gratitude to all of the people who have shared their stories with us over the years. Originally the idea was to conduct a simple study about what people feel is positive about their LGBTQ identities. We planned to share the results in a few academic papers and move on to the next project. This book is the product of the overwhelmingly positive response we received to our simple study idea and the requests to share our findings. It is our way of giving back (and paying it forward) to all of the LGBTQ people who have shared with us these stories from their amazing and inspiring lives.

It is a part of our privilege to claim our LGBTQ identities. We, within this particular time and culture, can claim these labels as a positive way to describe something about ourselves. We enjoy sufficient freedom to explore our sexual and gender identities. We have the opportunity and privilege to discover our feelings and claim identities that communicate a sense of who we are. With this privilege comes the responsibility to use our personal and social power to make the world a better place for others. All of us can use whatever privilege we have to encourage and affirm others as they claim their LGBTQ identities and as they seek to live their lives authentically and fully.

The people quoted in this book are just ordinary folks, like you and me. They are not celebrities (as far as we know!). It is great to have visible role models accessible on television, the Internet, in books, and movies. But the best role models are often the people we find right next door, in our neighborhoods, schools, places of worship, community organizations, and workplaces. The LGBTQ people who have shared their stories with us are extraordinary in the sense that they are living each day as well as they can. They strive to live positively with integrity and courage and optimism and compassion. We hope that you find inspiration in their stories.

Let's cultivate a positive view of LGBTQ identities. Let's start a new conversation and focus on embracing our identities and enhancing our well-being. Let's move forward with a positive narrative for our lives.

NOTES

CHAPTER 1

1. The letters LGBTQ as we use them technically stand for lesbian, gay, bisexual, transgender, and queer. For some people, especially those who may be uncomfortable with the word *queer* (we recognize that this word is still sometimes used in hateful and hurtful ways), Q may stand for questioning. We are fine with that. Participants in our studies have used the word *queer* to define their identities when they feel this word best describes an identity that they embrace. We use all of these terms in the broadest and most inclusive sense. You will see as you read this book, the people we have interviewed describe themselves in just about as many ways as there are people. For example, for some the term *transgender* may refer to their "genderqueer" identity as being between or beyond the two sexes (male/female). For others, *transgender* may refer to a past incongruence of their body appearance and their authentic sex as male or female. This incongruence may have been addressed or is in the process of being addressed, and what they share with us are the lessons they learned and the strengths they built through this process. All of these words and personally constructed meanings are within the purview of this book.

2. Analyses of recent survey samples report that the majority of those who identify as gay (men) or lesbian are in relationships. For example, unpublished analysis of our own data from a 2006 survey of a sample of more than 2,500 gay men and lesbians finds that 55 percent of the gay men report being in a committed relationship (and more than 60 percent of lesbians). A recent Metlife report (*Still Out, Still Aging*, downloadable at www.metlife.com/mmi/index.html) found that 61 percent of their sample of 1,201 self-identified LGBT individuals aged 45 to 64 reported being in a relationship. In short, plenty of contemporary evidence exists to debunk the negative stereotype.

3. Many books, documentaries, articles, and websites have positive stories of LGBTQ lives. For example, we enjoyed reading the stories of forty-four LGBTQ Americans interviewed by Philip Gambone (2010). Several of the websites in our Resources section include ways to find positive, inspiring stories.

4. Positive identity development is an important goal for LGBTQ people. Those who seek out therapeutic services cite this as their major goal (e.g., Liddle, 1996; Page, 2007). Talking about the strengths and joys of LGBTQ identities is an important part of the process of cultivating positive identity (see Godfrey, Haddock, Fisher, and Lund, 2006).

5. We believe that non-LGBTQ people can learn many lessons about positive identity and strength from LGBTQ people. In general, we take the view that the vast majority of people want to experience positive affect and a sense of well-being (for a review of the literature supporting this view, see Watson and Naragon, 2009). Non-LGBTQ people can learn from and be inspired by the experiences of LGBTQ people as we all develop and grow into an inclusive, diverse human community.

6. We hope that you will find something in this book that is helpful to you. We recognize, however, that every person is unique and has unique needs, goals, and approaches to life. Therefore, this book is informational only and not intended as a substitute for professional services that can be personalized for the individual or couple. It is important to note that for some people, exercises that focus on positivity may not be helpful or may even be counterproductive. If you feel that this is the case for you, if an exercise doesn't "feel right," then move on to the next exercise. Different approaches work for different people. That is one reason we include a variety of exercises.

7. The three articles were written using the four data sets analyzed separately. For this book, we combined the data sets and reanalyzed the data. Many of the same themes emerged again. Other themes were combined or are presented in a different way in this book. Some of the quotes from participants appear in both the articles and in this book. In this book, participant quotes are derived from the original data and not from the articles. The citations for the articles are Riggle, Whitman, Olson, Rostosky, and Strong (2008); Rostosky, Riggle, Pascale-Hague, and McCants (2010); Riggle, Rostosky, McCants, and Pascale-Hague (2011).

8. For example, see Cheng and Lee (2009) for a discussion of research on how asking about positive experiences related to racial and ethnic minority identity can facilitate positive identity development and integration of multiple identities.

9. When we looked up the definition of *conventional* using Google, the first two meanings were quite applicable to the way we use the term in this book: "1. Based on or in accordance with what is generally done or believed; 2. Concerned with what is generally held to be acceptable at the expense of individuality and sincerity."

10. For an interesting discussion of LGBT identity labels, and whether or not they are all under the same "umbrella," see Fassinger and Arseneau (2007).

11. For one example of the myriad labels and different meanings for the same label, see Eliason and Morgan (1998) for a nice enumeration of the different ways lesbians define themselves.

12. The self-descriptions that people provide in response to open-ended questions appear in quotation marks in the text. For simplicity, where people simply checked a box

in response to questions about their sexual, sex, and gender identities, we simply report these answers without quotation marks.

13. For example, see Bowleg (2008).

14. Specific findings from this research can be found in the following journal articles: Dudley et al. (2005); Rostosky, Riggle, Dudley, and Comer Wright (2006); Rostosky, Riggle, Gray, and Hatton (2007); Rostosky et al. (2008).

15. Specific findings from this research can be found in the following journal articles: Rostosky and Riggle (2002); Rostosky et al. (2004).

16. For detailed information see the following journal articles: Riggle and Rostosky (2005); Riggle et al. (2006); Riggle, Rostosky, and Horne (2010b); Riggle, Rostosky, and Prather (2006).

17. Additional information about these studies can be found in Rostosky, Otis, Riggle, Kelley, and Brodnicki (2007); Rostosky, Riggle, Brodnicki, and Olson (2009).

18. Results from our research on marriage inequality and marriage restriction amendments to state constitutions can be found in the following articles: Fingerhut, Riggle, and Rostosky (2011); Horne, Rostosky, and Riggle (2011); Riggle, Thomas, and Rostosky (2005); Riggle, Rostosky, and Horne (2009); Rostosky, Riggle, Horne, and Miller (2009); Rostosky, Riggle, Horne, Denton, and Huellemeier (2010).

19. To read more about minority stress, see Brooks (1981); Meyer (2003).

20. See Meyer (2003).

21. For various discussions of these impacts, see Cochran (2001); Makadon, Mayer, Potter, and Goldhammer (2007); Meyer and Northridge (2007).

22. There are numerous books and articles on the general problem of bullying, especially focusing on the epidemic of bullying of young people in schools. For example, see Swearer, Espelage, and Napolitano (2009). For up-to-date information on research and resources, see GLSEN (Gay, Lesbian and Straight Education Network) at www.GLSEN.org.

23. The messages of hope portrayed in the It Gets Better campaign can help to inspire and empower young LGBTQ people (and their families and allies). The It Gets Better videos are available online. A related book of personal stories is also available (Savage and Miller, 2010).

24. Several reports from surveys conducted by GLSEN point to the problem of inadequate training or resources for school personnel to deal with bullying. Although the vast majority of teachers say that bullying of LGBTQ youth is problematic, many also underestimate the extent of the problem and its impact. Go to the website of GLSEN for more information (www.GLSEN.org).

25. See, for example, Riggle, Rostosky, and Horne (2010a).

26. For an overview of the psychological research on meaning making, see Steger (2009).

27. This book includes quotes that make comparisons between LGBTQ people and straight or heterosexual people. There are also quotes that include reference to "men" and "women" in general. The use of generalities, and even stereotypes, is intended by the participant to make a point. We hope that the reader takes these comments in the spirit in which they are intended—making a point about a positive aspect of LGBTQ identities—and not as a negative comment about others.

28. For more information on Frank Kameny and his many contributions to LGBTQ rights, go to the Kameny Papers website (www.kamenypapers.org).

29. See Constantine and Sue (2006).

30. We want the reader to experience a sense of connection to the people telling their stories in this book; however, we don't use proper names in the examples in the following chapters. There are a couple of important reasons. First, using names that are typical for people of European descent (especially names with English origins) can erase a person's ethnic origins. But at the same time, if we tried to use names to reflect an ethnic origin (which we only sometimes know about our participants), we might fairly be criticized for using stereotypical names. Second, as we note in chapter 4, names are often seen as denoting a male person or a female person. For example, when you read the story about "M.J." at the beginning of this chapter, did you automatically assume that the two coworkers were male because we gave them the names "John" and "David"? Most people would, and that is how we envisioned them, but it is not necessary to the story. By using names that are typically seen as "male" we created an assumption. What about M.J.? Did you make any assumptions about the person with that name? We intentionally used this name to create an ambiguity. Is this person male or female or transgender? Does it matter? We want you, the reader, to relate to all of the storytellers in this book. So make up your own names and images. We leave that to your vast creativity.

CHAPTER 2

1. For a recent general review of the concepts of self and identity in psychological research, see Swann and Bosson (2010).

2. Creating narratives about who we are and how we came to our present identity is important to how we understand ourselves. In turn, these stories support our sense of well-being. For example, King, Burton, and Geise (2009) examine how coming-out stories may help us to understand our social interactions with others around our identity and how we build a "good gay life."

3. Park, Peterson, and Seligman (2004) define authenticity as "speaking the truth and presenting oneself in a genuine way" (p. 606).

4. A sense of well-being comes from having the autonomy to discover who we are as individuals and then interact authentically in all the spheres of our lives. See, for example, Ryff (1989).

5. See Harter (2005).

6. For an interesting discussion of how LGBTQQA (lesbian, gay, bisexual, transgender, queer, questioning, and allies) people construct their identities with "integrity," see Moorhead (1999).

7. For example, courage is an important life skill. Although the word is commonly used, researchers are just now distinguishing between different types of courage and how they are related to our well-being. For a review, see Pury and Lopez (2009).

8. There are many so-called coming-out models. Cass's (1979) six-stage model of gay and lesbian identity formation may be one of the most well-known and cited. However, there are many other models, such as Fassinger's (1998) four-phase model. Fassinger's model includes both individual identity and one's identification with the group. There are many astute critiques of these models and others as scholars continue to try to improve our understanding of the coming-out process.

Models of transgender identity development discuss the unique opportunities that transgender identity may present for finding meaning in life (e.g., Lev, 2004, 2007; Maguen, Shipherd, Harris, and Welch, 2007). Bradford's (2004) stage model of bisexual identity development notes that a sense of community makes a positive contribution to life satisfaction. Other general models of the development of positive identity are included in Makadon et al. (2007).

9. See Cass (1979); Fassinger (1998).

10. For a general discussion of this connection, see Harter (2005).

11. For example, see Swigonski (1995).

12. King (2008), p. 439.

13. Carl Rogers (1977) maintained that all human beings have a self-actualizing tendency that leads to positive psychological growth and healthy relationships with others. A necessary ingredient is an environment that supports growth.

14. Many resources are available to allies of LGBTQ people. One of the most accessible is the website of PFLAG (Parents and Friends of Lesbians and Gays: www.PFLAG.org). Despite the name, this group is also for allies of bisexual and transgender individuals. The Safe Schools Coalition has many resources for being an ally for school-age children and young adults (www.safeschoolscoalition.org). For research on being an ally in the workplace, see Hall (2009). For research on why and how non-LGBT people become allies, see Duhigg, Rostosky, Gray, and Wimsatt (2010).

15. Models of transgender identity suggest that developing congruency between inner experiences of sex or gender and external expressions is an important step toward self-acceptance and positive identity development. For examples of these models, see Finnegan and McNally (2002); Kaufman (2008).

CHAPTER 3

1. For one review of the "coming-out" literature and an example of how it may lead to positive identity, see Greenfield (2008).

2. For a general discussion of this process, see Park, Peterson, and Seligman (2004).

3. See Fassinger (1998); Abes and Jones (2004). Cognitive complexity refers to multidimensional thinking that allows us to analyze several relationships at once. Abes and Jones (2004) use this term to point out that cognitive complexity is a skill; learning to think in this higher-order way allows us to differentiate our identity from the identity of others and create our own new identity. While their research was limited to participants who identified as gay or lesbian, we believe that people who identify as

bisexual, transgender, and queer may also develop cognitive complexity through the same process.

4. For nice overviews of these general concepts, see Goleman (1997, 2006) or see a review of the literature in Salovey, Mayer, Caruso, and Yoo (2009).

5. Retrieved from http://allpsych.com/dictionary/dictionary2.html.

6. See Thorndike (2007).

7. Ryff (1989) identified "positive relations with others" and "environmental mastery" as important factors in our sense of well-being.

8. See Loevinger (1976). Ego development has also been linked to openness to experience, compassion, and empathy (Helson and Roberts, 1994).

9. Ego development and strength comes from actively struggling to make sense out of difficult experiences, which results in insight (Bauer and McAdams, 2004; King, 2001).

10. See Ryff (1989) for a discussion of the general importance of self-acceptance, autonomy, and personal growth to well-being.

11. A "benefit-finding" perspective on life may lead to personal growth. That is, we can find our strengths in facing the stresses and challenges of life. See Lechner, Tennen, and Affleck (2009) for a brief review of the research on this topic.

12. See Brown (1989).

13. See Brown (1989, p. 449).

14. See Helminiak (2008). Also, for a general discussion of the role of spirituality in well-being, see Peterson and Seligman (2004).

15. Although many LGBTQ people may be skeptical about organized religions because of negative experiences with churches or negative rhetoric reported in the press, researchers have found that spirituality, religion, and faith are important in the lives of a majority of LGBTQ people. Finding a way to express and practice religious or faith traditions in a supportive environment may present challenges, but when found may contribute to a sense of well-being. For example, research by Lease, Horne, and Noffsinger-Frazier (2005) finds that experiencing "high levels of affirmation at their places of worship" (p. 384) is associated with better psychological health for LGB individuals. For those who wish to find affirmative faith experiences, there are many affinity groups associated with larger religious traditions as well as a growing number of "open and affirming" churches in many denominations.

16. See Gilley (2006), Jacobs, Wesley, and Lang (1997), and Roscoe (1998) for some historic and current perspectives on two-spirit cultures.

17. Adapted from Hill (2004).

18. For exercises related to writing a "spiritual autobiography," see Astramovich (2003).

CHAPTER 4

1. While there are many books on this topic, one of the early and still-provocative discussions is found in Fausto-Sterling (2000a).

2. A "social norm" is something that is customary or widespread in a society. These norms include rules for how to act within particular social situations or interactions. People are pressured to conform to norms, and they are sanctioned or penalized for not conforming. For a classic review of some of the psychological literature on social norms, see Cialdini and Trost (1998).

3. Fausto-Sterling (2000b) has written about the complexity of sex (and gender). She suggests it is erroneous to think of sex and gender as dichotomies or as a continuum with two "opposite" poles (male and female). Instead, sex and gender are complex, diverse, multidimensional configurations of genetic, hormonal, anatomical, and environmental (social) influences. For more information about intersexed persons, one website to check out is the Intersex Society of North America (www.isna.org).

4. For an encyclopedic collection (literally!) of the differences in how women/girls and men/boys are socialized and treated, see Worrell (2001).

5. For a review of psychological research on gender identity, gender socialization, gender roles, and gender in the social context, see Wood and Eagly (2010).

6. For example, appreciating human diversity (e.g., going beyond the binaries and norms) is a basis for building an expanded social support network. This is valuable to our sense of well-being. For a discussion, see Godfrey et al. (2006); Rust (2002).

7. Positive beliefs and the skill of creating meaning help us to be flexible and creative thinkers and increase our well being (see Tulgade and Fredrickson, 2007).

8. See Simonsen, Blazina, and Watkins (2000).

9. See Abes and Jones (2004).

10. See Sanger (2008); Rubin (2006).

11. See Brown (1989).

12. Retrieved from http://dictionary.reference.com/browse/queer.

13. For the original treatise on compulsory heterosexuality, see Rich (1980).

14. See a review of the literature on gay and lesbian parents in Goldberg (2009).

15. See Ochs and Rowley (2009).

16. This exercise is adapted from Remer and Remer (2000).

17. This exercise is adapted from Mejía (2005).

CHAPTER 5

1. There are many books, articles, and reviews on the relationships of LGBTQ people to their families of origin. For some examples in the psychological literature, see Ritter and Terndrup (2002); Lev (2004) includes discussion of relationships between transgender individuals and their families; see Scherrer (2010) for an interesting review of relationships between grandparents and LGBQ grandchildren.

2. For a recent review of literature and an excellent study of parent-child relationships, see Goldberg (2009).

3. For an interesting study of how gay men and lesbians construct their friendships as they age, see de Vries and Megathlin (2009; this entire issue of the *Journal of GLBT*

Family Studies [vol. 5, issue 1/2] is devoted to the intersection of LGBT aging and family and community).

Strong social support networks, regardless of composition, are important to our emotional and physical health, especially for LGBTQ people (Barker, Herdt, and de Vries, 2006).

4. For a general review of the psychological literature related to belonging, see Leary (2008). To read about the importance of positive relationships with others to our well-being, see Ryff (1989).

5. See Miller and Stiver (1991). The work of Jean Baker Miller and other relational-cultural psychologists is summarized in a book by Robb (2006).

6. See Ryff and Keyes (1995).

7. For example, a study of transsexual-identified individuals finds benefits from social support from family (Erich, Tittsworth, Dykes, and Cabuses, 2008; also, for transsexuals of color, supportive social networks are especially important; see Erich, Tittsworth, and Kersten, 2010).

8. See Russell and Richards (2003).

9. See Duhigg et al. (2010).

10. See Rumens (2010); Huffman, Watrous-Brodriguez, and King (2008).

11. See Levant and Richmond (2007).

12. See Fingerhut, Peplau, and Ghavami (2005).

13. See Diener and Seligman (2002).

14. See Rostosky et al. (2004).

15. For a review of thirteen studies of factors related to coming out to parents and effects of disclosure, see Heatherington and Lavner (2008). For many LGBTQ people, after disclosure the quality of family relationships may initially suffer but over time return to the same levels as before disclosure or the relationships improve. Whether family relationships improve or not depends on a number of complex and interacting individual and family-level factors that are not under the direct control of the person who is coming out. These factors include parents' attitudes and beliefs, gender and ethnicity of parents, gender of child, and how adaptable and cohesive the family is.

16. See Otis, Rostosky, Riggle, and Hamrin (2006).

17. See Gates, Badgett, Macomer, and Chambers (2007); Grant et al. (2011). We have been unable to locate current comparable studies of bisexual or queer-identified persons, pointing to the need for future study.

18. See Weston (1991) and Oswald (2002).

19. Our intimate relationships give our life meaning and purpose. For example, Sang (1993) found that intimate relationships and friendships give meaning and satisfaction to the lives of midlife lesbians.

20. See Imber-Black (2003).

21. See Fredrickson, Cohn, Coffey, Pek, and Finkel (2008); Hutcherson, Seppala, and Gross (2008).

CHAPTER 6

1. There are literally thousands of articles and books on the use of gender, sex, and sexual stereotypes in media (including television, film, the Internet, and print media). Scholars analyze the messages that are relayed to adults and children about how men and women should act. Some of these articles and books include discussion of how deviations from the "norms" are seen as humorous but are not serious attempts to create new rules for men and women. The following citations are just a sample of the scholarship that is available: Carnes (2001); King, Bloodsworth-Lugo; Lugo-Lugo (2010); Lemish (2008); and Scharrer, Kim, Lin, and Liu (2006).

2. For a review of the benefits of curiosity, see Kashdan and Silvia (2009).

3. There are also thousands of articles and books about the positive effects that intimate relationships can have on partners (e.g., Carroll, 2010; Gottman et al., 2003). For a general review of psychological research on intimate relationships, see Berscheid and Reis (1998); for a general update of this research, see Clark and Lemay (2010).

4. For a review, see Hendrick and Hendrick (2009); Maisel and Gable (2009).

5. For one of many books on the topic, see Hendrick and Hendrick (2000).

6. See Rostosky et al. (2006).

7. See Brown (1989, p.452).

8. See Berger and Kelly (1986); Friend (1987, 1990).

9. See Ritter and Terndrup (2002, p. 141).

10. Several review articles are available about children with gay and lesbian parents. One of the most recent and comprehensive is Goldberg (2009). For discussions of the similarities (and differences) between heterosexual and same-sex relationships, see Balsam, Beauchaine, Rothblum, and Solomon (2008); Kurdek (2004); Mackey, Diemer, and O'Brien (2004); Solomon, Rothblum, and Balsam (2004, 2005).

11. For one example of research on how lesbian couples negotiate equality in household roles, see Esmail (2010).

12. See Kurdek (2005, 2006); Peplau and Fingerhut (2007).

13. See Kurdek (2005, 2006); Solomon, Rothblum, and Balsam (2005).

14. See DeMaris (2007); Helms, Proulx, Klute, McHale, and Crouter (2006); Wood (2010).

15. There is a lively debate about the concept of fluidity of sexual orientation (e.g., Diamond, 2008) and gender and sex identity (e.g., Bernstein, 2006; Bornstein and Bergman, 2010; Nestle, Wilchins, and Howell, 2002).

CHAPTER 7

1. For a review of the concept of compassion in positive psychology, see Cassell (2009). Wachholtz and Pearce (2007) offer a slightly more complex definition: "[Compassion is] a multifaceted concept involving the direction of kind awareness to another,

a perception of the other's suffering, a desire to relieve the suffering, and subsequent action to do so" (p. 126).

2. For a general overview of how empathy may lead to altruism (an enhanced feeling of connection and responsibility toward others), see Batson, Ahmad, and Lishner (2009).

3. See a summary of this research in Walchholtz and Pearce (2007).

4. The concept of "The Wounded Healer" has roots in Greek mythology, ancient shamanism, and show up again in modern psychoanalysis. See Stone (2008).

5. See Van Keelf et al. (2008).

6. See Johnson (2003, p. 153).

7. Rosenblum and Travis (2008) note, "There is probably nothing more fundamental to social change than learning who you are, finding and honoring that authentic self, recognizing that it is multifaceted, complex, *and evolving*—and then making sure that the social change methods you use are consistent with that self" (p. 470).

8. For a brief review of the psychological research on "uniqueness," how it is related to group identification, and how it can help to enhance our well-being, see Lynn and Snyder (2005).

9. See Palmer (1998).

10. See Brown (1989).

11. See Davidson and Harrington (2002).

12. See Carson, Carson, Gil, and Baucom (2004); Steffen and Masters (2005).

13. This exercise was adapted from Wachholtz and Pearce (2007).

CHAPTER 8

1. Many theorists have written that "self-transcendence" helps to give our life meaning. For two examples, see Allport (1961) and Seligman (2002).

2. LGBTQ role models are becoming more accessible and visible in the media. This visibility has a positive impact on the formation of LGBTQ identities (Gomillion and Biuliano, 2011).

3. See Dillon (1999).

4. Engaging with others in significant and meaningful ways brings positive feelings and benefits for our well-being (Nakamura and Csikszentmihalyi, 2003).

5. Erik Erikson (1980, 1982), a developmental psychologist, observed that middle adulthood was a particularly important developmental period for focusing on caring for future generations.

6. See Russell and Horne (2009).

7. A qualitative study of the adolescent children of lesbian mothers (O'Connell, 1999), for instance, noted that the adolescents perceived substantial benefits to their own development and a very positive relationship with their mothers. The benefits the adolescents perceived included learning to be more open-minded and less judgmental. They also appreciated that their mothers had modeled the courage to take the risks to live authentically and honestly.

8. See Rostosky, Riggle, Dudley, and Wright (2006).

9. See Kurdek (2004, 2008); Mackey, Diemer, and O'Brien (2004); Roisman, Clausell, Holland, Fortuna, and Elief (2008).

10. See Rostosky, Riggle, Gray, and Hatton (2007).

11. See a review of this research in Rothblum (2009).

12. See Rostosky, Riggle, Dudley, and Wright (2006).

13. See Rothblum (2009).

14. See Waterman (1993).

15. See Zimmerman (1995).

16. See Russell, Muraco, Subramaniam, and Laub (2009).

17. See Adler (1964).

18. See Cohler, Hostetler, and Boxer (1998); Sang (1993).

19. See McAdams, Diamond, de St. Aubin, and Mansfield (1997).

20. Some of the same qualities (listed in this book) that LGBTQ people see as positive about our identities may lend themselves to making LGBTQ people good (and even excellent) leaders in a variety of settings (Fassinger, Shullman, and Stevenson, 2010).

21. See Seligman, Steen, Park, and Peterson (2005).

22. See Frisch (2006).

23. See Frisch (2006).

CHAPTER 9

1. LGBTQ people have different experiences within the LGBTQ community (see Fassinger and Arseneau, 2007). Some of these differences are based on sex or gender; other differences are based on sexual orientation or attraction; yet others are based on racial, ethnic, or cultural identities. For examples, see Hines, (2007, 2010); Lehavot, Balsam, and Ibrahim-Wells, (2009); Sanger, (2008).

2. See Galliher, Rostosky, and Hughes (2004); Rostosky, Owens, Zimmerman, and Riggle (2003).

3. Esther Rothblum (2010) defines the LGBT[Q] community as "LGBT[Q] individuals or organizations with whom one has perceived similarity due to sexual orientation, and who provide connection with others, recreation, and/or support."

4. For discussions of the impact of community on the development of sexual or gender identity, see examples in Firestein (2007); Haldeman (2007); Lev (2007); Liddle (2007); Potocznlak, (2007).

5. See Deci and Ryan (2000); Diener (2000).

6. Out & Equal (www.outandequal.org) provides information on "best practices" for businesses.

7. See Ochs and Rowley (2009).

8. There has been research on community connections within each of these separate communities. For example, LeBeau and Jellison (2009) studied how gay and bisexual men related to the "gay community" and its impact on their identity.

9. See Lehavot, Balsam, and Ibrahim-Wells (2009).

10. See Lehavot, Balsam, and Ibrahim-Wells (2009).

11. Russell and Richards (2003) identified five basic resilience factors for LGB people who had experienced an antigay referendum in Colorado in 1992 [Amendment 2 to the state constitution, which denied lesbian, gay, and bisexual-identified people legal recourse for discrimination; since overturned by the United States Supreme Court in Romer v. Evans, 517 U.S. 620 (1996)]. These resilience factors included both the interaction and support that they had experienced within the LGB community and an expanded perspective on the LGB rights movement (and civil rights more broadly). Other research has found that interaction with the LGBTQ community is a source of support during antigay political events, such as marriage restriction amendment campaigns (e.g., Rostosky et al., 2010).

12. See Harper and Schneider (2003).

CHAPTER 10

1. See Lefcourt (2005).

2. We talk about optimism after the marriage restriction campaigns in 2006 more extensively in Rostosky et al. (2010).

3. For a general review of how optimism positively impacts well-being, see Peterson and Chang (2003). Also see Carver, Scheier, Miller, and Fulford (2009).

4. Several writers have explored the meaning of "optimal human functioning" for persons of color in the United States, most notably psychologist Derald Wing Sue. For example, Sue and Constantine (2003) discuss "the whiteness dimensions" of how optimal human functioning is typically talked about by psychologists and how the difference in values endorsed by different racial and ethnic groups affects optimal functioning. They caution against the harms of overgeneralization.

5. See See Bowleg, Craig, and Burkholder (2004); Bowleg, Huang, Brooks, Black, and Burkholder, (2003); Wilson and Miller (2002); Zea, Reisen, and Poppen (1999).

6. For example, see McLelland, Suganuma, and Welker (2007); Simon and Brooks (2009).

7. For example, the academic journal *Sexuality Research and Social Policy* has published several special issues on the constructions and definitions of sexualities, including same-sex sexualities, in minority cultures in the United States and in many other countries in the world. For other examples, see Asencio and Battle (2010); Laboy, Sandfort, and Yi (2009).

8. Dahlsgaard, Peterson, and Seligman (2005) find certain virtues are present in many cultures of the world. These common virtues are wisdom, courage, humanity, justice, temperance, and transcendence. Park, Peterson, and Seligman (2006) similarly found that the "most commonly endorsed strengths" across forty countries are "kindness, fairness, authenticity, gratitude, and open-mindedness."

SUGGESTED RESOURCES

The number of books, movies, websites, support groups, and organizations for LGBTQ-identified people and their allies is vast and constantly growing. Just a quick search online will quickly uncover an overwhelming amount of information. We include just a few of these many available resources (we try to provide an idea of the mission of the organization where appropriate). We make no attempt to be exhaustive or even representative. We are not endorsing any particular group or website over another. The websites we suggest provide topical information and also list other resources to help you find additional materials. We hope that you find these helpful.

Several websites for organizations of helping professionals and social service providers have interesting and useful information for LGBTQ-identified people, their allies, and the professionals who serve them. You can access this information even if you are not a member of the organization.

WWW.APA.ORG

This is the website of the American Psychological Association (APA). APA works to end stigma and discrimination against LGBTQ-identified people and promote their well-being through solid science and scholar-ship, education, training, and advocacy. On this website, you can find links to many resources related to gender identity, sexual orientation, and sexuality. On the APA home page, you will find links to the LGBT Concerns Office, the Committee on LGBT Concerns, and several divi-sions that have LGBT interests, including School Psychology (Division 16), Counseling Psychology (Division 17), and the Society for the Psy-chological Study of LGBT Issues (Division 44). There are also impor-tant professional guidelines regarding service for LGBTQ individuals. APA has been active in supporting equality for LGBTQ people around the world, including supporting policies for equal parenting and mar-riage rights. This website includes several links to bibliographies of the psychological literature on LGBTQ issues.

WWW.SOCIALWORKERS.ORG

The National Association of Social Workers formed The National Com-mittee on Lesbian, Gay, Bisexual and Transgender Issues to develop, review, and monitor programs of the association that significantly affect gay men, lesbians, bisexuals, and transgender individuals. The Diversity & Equity link has a number of position statements and citations for papers on LGBT issues.

WWW.ALGBTIC.ORG

The Association for Lesbian, Gay, Bisexual, and Transgender Issues in Counseling (ALGBTIC) is a division of the American Counseling As-sociation. The website has many resources related to providing compe-tent, affirming, and culturally sensitive counseling services. ALGBTIC also publishes a newsletter and an academic publication titled *The Jour-nal of LGBT Issues in Counseling.*

WWW.AGLP.ORG

The Association of Gay and Lesbian Psychiatrists "educates and advo-cates" on LGBT mental health issues. Their website has links to many helpful resources.

There are also websites for other helping professionals, including the Gay and Lesbian Medical Association, www.glma.org, and the National LGBT Bar Association, www.lgbtbar.org. It is easy to search online and find organizations important to your interests.

Education-related services and assistance for LGBTQ identified and questioning adolescents and young adults are important. We list a few of the major organizations providing information.

WWW.GLSEN.ORG

The Gay, Lesbian and Straight Education Network (GLSEN) is a leading national education organization focused on ensuring safe schools for all students, regardless of sexual orientation or gender identity/expression. On this website, you can find tools and tips for educators and students to use in their schools to promote a school climate that respects and values diversity. These tools include workshop materials such as the GLSEN lunchbox, curriculum materials, safe space materials, and tips for starting a gay-straight alliance.

WWW.NEA-GLBTC.ORG

The Gay, Lesbian, Bisexual, Transgender Caucus of the National Education Association "works to provide GLBT teachers, education support professionals, and students, with safe schools free of anti-GLBT bias and intolerance, and to provide sound education programs for all students." They also provide training for educators on addressing GLBT bias and bullying in schools.

WWW.THETREVORPROJECT.ORG

The Trevor Project is a national organization providing crisis and suicide prevention services to lesbian, gay, bisexual, transgender, and questioning (LGBTQ) youth. Their website has information for educators and parents and links to other websites that serve LGBTQ-identified and questioning youth and young adults. This website hosts a chat line and a suicide hotline. Also, you can download an extensive list of books and films that are categorized for young gay men, young lesbians, young bisexuals, young transgender, gender-nonconforming, or questioning youth. Included in the list are books and films for everyone, including parents and teachers.

Resources to support equality in the workplace and professional networking groups can be found online. These organizations provide information about best business practices for supporting LGBTQ employees. We provide one example here.

WWW.OUTANDEQUAL.ORG

Out & Equal Workplace Advocates is a nonprofit organization dedicated to achieving workplaces where full equality extends to people of all sexual orientations and gender identities. On this website, you can find a Career Resource Center as well as information about diversity training and ally development in the workplace. Additional resources on this website include information on LGBT youth, marriage equality, and diverse cultural communities.

Many local, national, and international organizations support LGBTQ rights. We list three of the large, national organizations. We urge you to find your local or state organizations through a web search.

WWW.HRC.ORG

The Human Rights Campaign (HRC) is "the largest national lesbian, gay, bisexual and transgender civil rights organization. HRC envisions an America where LGBT people are ensured of their basic equal rights, and can be open, honest and safe at home, at work and in the community." Web pages are devoted to issues such as aging, religion and faith, parenting, marriage, military, people of color, youth and campus activism, transgender, health, international rights and immigration, coming out, and workplace issues. A variety of resources and publications are available on these pages for LGBTQ people and their allies.

WWW.ACLU.ORG/LGBT-RIGHTS

The American Civil Liberties Union LGBT Project "fights discrimination and moves public opinion through the courts, legislatures and public education across five issue areas: Relationships, Youth & Schools, Parenting, Gender Identity and Expression, and Discrimination in Employment, Housing and other areas." This web page has extensive information on legal issues and court cases in each of these five areas.

WWW.THETASKFORCE.ORG

The National Gay and Lesbian Task Force supports the building of grassroots organizations and groups in the LGBT communities. This website has a wealth of information on many issues that affect the LGBTQ community, including aging, faith, hate crimes, health, youth, marriage, parenting, and racial and economic justice. There are also specific pages providing information on bisexual and transgender issues.

Support for allies of the LGBTQ community is important. One of the most well-known groups is PFLAG.

WWW.PFLAG.ORG

Parents, Friends, and Families of Lesbians and Gays (PFLAG) promotes "the health and well-being of lesbian, gay, bisexual and transgender persons, their families and friends through: support, to cope with an adverse society; education, to enlighten an ill-informed public; and advocacy, to end discrimination and to secure equal civil rights. [PFLAG] provides opportunity for dialogue about sexual orientation and gender identity, and acts to create a society that is healthy and respectful of human diversity." Resources on this website include information about the Families of Color Network, Affirming Faith Communities, Safe Schools, and Advocacy training. Information on current issues such as the military, relationship recognition, and bullying is also available.

The following websites are for a wide variety of organizations or information sources. We remind you that this is but a small sample from a really big buffet. If you have a particular interest, there is most likely a website that serves that interest.

WWW.BINETUSA.ORG

BiNet "collects and distributes educational information regarding sexual orientation and gender identity with an emphasis on the bisexual and pansexual and allied communities." Social networking, reading lists, and academic resources are available on this website.

WWW.NBJC.ORG

"The National Black Justice Coalition (NBJC) is a civil rights organization dedicated to empowering Black lesbian, gay, bisexual, and transgender (LGBT) people. NBJC's mission is to eradicate racism and homophobia. As America's leading national Black LGBT civil rights organization focused on federal public policy, the National Black Justice Coalition has accepted the charge to lead Black families in strengthening the bonds and bridging the gaps between straight and LGBT people and communities." This website has some excellent papers on marriage equality, welcoming congregations, theology, and interviews with prominent and influential LGBT African Americans and Allies.

WWW.DEAFQUEER.ORG

The Deaf Queer Resource Center provides information for the Deaf Lesbian, Gay, Bisexual, Transgender, Transsexual, Intersex, and Questioning communities.

WWW.QUEERASIANSPIRIT.ORG

"Queer Asian Spirit is a not-for-profit organization, dedicated to affirming and supporting the spiritual lives of lesbian, gay, bisexual, transgen-

der, and queer (LGBTQ) people of Asian descent everywhere." This
website lists hundreds of resources from many faith traditions and faith
communities around the world.

WWW.SOULFORCE.ORG

"Soulforce is committed to freedom for lesbian, gay, bisexual, transgender, and queer people from religious and political oppression
through relentless nonviolent resistance." The website describes various
Soulforce-sponsored campaigns, including the Equality Ride that trains
young activists in nonviolent resistance and visits educational institutions across the nation. The resource page has information on LGBTQ
identity from the perspective of scientific research and theology. There
are also links to many other helpful organizations and resources for engaging in mutually respectful dialogues.

WWW.NATIVEOUT.COM

NativeOUT is a "national nonprofit education and media organization,
actively involved in the Two Spirit Movement. Our vision is to create
social change in rural and urban communities that benefit Indigenous
Lesbian, Gay, Bisexual, Transgender, Queer, and Two Spirit people."
There are many interesting resources, including videos, available on
this website.

WWW.NTAC.ORG

The National Transgender Center provides resources for the transgen-
der community, including resources for coming out and finding support.
This site also provides links to advocacy groups, such as the Renaissance
Transgender Association, Transgender Law and Policy Institute, the
International Foundation for Gender Education, and the American
Educational Gender Information Service, among others.

WWW.TRANSEQUALITY.ORG

The National Center for Transgender Equality is "dedicated to the equality of transgender people through advocacy, collaboration and empowerment." The resources page has information about transgender people, building community, federal issues, and how to become involved in the political process.

WWW.ROBYNOCHS.COM

Robyn Ochs collected stories in a book called *Getting Bi: Voices of Bisexuals Around the World*. She is a popular speaker. Her website has a wealth of resources including an extensive list of fiction, biography, and poetry that in some way focuses on bisexual behavior and/or bisexual identity. Her resources page also has links to other websites that focus on LGBTQ, transgender, bisexual, intersex, youth, marriage equality, and other important issues.

WWW.ISNA.ORG

"The Intersex Society of North America (ISNA) is devoted to systemic change to end shame, secrecy, and unwanted genital surgeries for people born with an anatomy that someone decided is not standard for male or female." This website provides information on intersexuality and a variety of resources including bibliographies.

And if you are just looking for some people with similar interests to have fun with, try one of these organizations, or find the organization for LGBTQ people who share your interests. There are groups out there for almost any kind of hobby or fun activity. For example, you might want to try the International Gay Bowling Association (www. igbo.org), International Gay and Lesbian Outdoor Organizations (www.hikinglite.com/igloo), International Gay Rodeo Association (www.igra.org), or, if you like to sing, the GALA Choruses website will help you to find your local GLBT choruses (www.galachoruses. org). Websites for a variety of local groups also exist. For example, local reading groups, social discussion groups, or political groups can be found through a search of the web or links from other websites. These groups can be a great way to find and engage with others who have similar interests.

REFERENCES

Abes, E. S., and Jones, S. R. (2004). Meaning-making capacity and the dynamics of lesbian college students' multiple dimensions of identity. *Journal of College Student Development, 45*(6), 612–32.

Adler, A. (1964). Advantages and disadvantages of the inferiority feeling. In H. L. Ansbacher and R. R. Ansbacher (Eds.), *Superiority and social interest: A collection of later writings* (pp. 29–40). Evanston, IL: Northwestern University Press. (Original work published 1933.)

Allport, G. W. (1961). *Pattern and growth in personality.* New York, NY: Holt, Rinehart & Winston.

Asencio, M., and Battle, J. (2010). Special issue: Black and Latina/o sexualities. *Sexuality Research and Social Policy, 7*(2), 67–69.

Astramovich, R. L. (2003). Facilitating spiritual wellness with gays, lesbians, and bisexuals: Composing a spiritual autobiography. In J. S. Whitman and C. J. Boyd (Eds.), *The therapist's notebook for lesbian, gay, and bisexual clients: Homework, handouts, and activities for use in psychotherapy* (pp. 210–14). New York, NY: Haworth.

Balsam, K. F., Beauchaine, T. P., Rothblum, E. D., and Solomon, S. E. (2008). Three-year follow-up of same-sex couples who had civil unions in Vermont, same-sex couples not in civil unions, and heterosexual married couples. *Developmental Psychology, 44,* 102–16.

Barker, J. C., Herdt, G., and de Vries, B. (2006). Social support in the lives of lesbians and gay men at midlife and later. *Sexuality Research and Social Policy, 3,* 1–23.

Batson, C. D., Ahmad, N., and Lishner, D. A. (2009). Empathy and altruism. In C. R. Snyder and S. J. Lopez (Eds.), *Oxford handbook of positive psychology* (pp. 417–26). New York, NY: Oxford University.

Bauer, J. J., and McAdams, D. P. (2004). Growth goals, maturity, and well-being. *Developmental Psychology, 40*, 114–27.

Berger, R. M., and Kelly, J. J. (1986). Working with homosexuals of the older population. *Social Casework, 67*, 203–10.

Bernstein, M. (Ed.) (2006). *Nobody passes: Rejecting the rules of gender and conformity*. Berkeley, CA: Seal Press.

Berscheid, E., and Reis, H. T. (1998). Attraction and close relationships. In D. T. Gilbert, S. T. Fiske, and G. Lindzey (Eds.), *The handbook of social psychology*, Vol. 2, 4th ed. (pp. 193–281). Boston, MA: McGraw-Hill.

Bornstein, K., and Bergman, S. B. (2010). *Gender outlaws: The next generation*. Berkeley, CA: Seal Press.

Bowleg, L. (2008). When Black + Woman + Lesbian? ≠ Black Lesbian Woman: The methodological challenges of qualitative and quantitative intersectionality research. *Sex Roles, 59*(5–6), 312–25.

Bowleg, L., Craig, M. L., and Burkholder, G. (2004). Rising and surviving: A conceptual model of active coping among black lesbians. *Cultural Diversity and Ethnic Minority Psychology, 10*, 229–40.

Bowleg, L., Huang, J., Brooks, K., Black, A., and Burkholder, G. (2003). Triple jeopardy and beyond: Multiple minority stress and resilience among black lesbians. *Journal of Lesbian Studies, 7*, 87–108.

Bradford, M. (2004). The bisexual experience: Living in a dichotomous culture. *Journal of Bisexuality, 4*, 7–23.

Brooks, V. R. (1981). *Minority stress and lesbian women*. Lexington, MA: Lexington Books.

Brown, L. S. (1989). New voices, new visions: Toward a lesbian/gay paradigm for psychology. *Psychology of Women Quarterly, 13*, 445–58.

Carnes, M. (2001). Humor. In J. Worrell (Ed.), *Encyclopedia of women and gender: Sex similarities and differences and the impact of society on gender, Volume 1* (pp. 601–10). Burlington, MA: Elsevier Science and Technology Books.

Carroll, J. L. (2010). *Sexuality now: Embracing diversity*. Belmont, CA: Wadsworth Cengage Learning.

Carson, J. W., Carson, K. M., Gil, K. M., and Baucom, D. H. (2004). Mindfulness-based relationship enhancement. *Behavior Therapy, 35*, 471–94.

Carver, C. S., Scheier, M. F., Miller, C. J., and Fulford, D. (2009). Optimism. In C. R. Snyder and S. J. Lopez (Eds.), *Oxford handbook of positive psychology* (pp. 207–15). New York, NY: Oxford University.

Cass, V. (1979). Homosexual identity formation: A theoretical model. *Journal of Homosexuality, 4*(3), 219–35.

Cassell, E. J. (2009). Compassion. In C. R. Snyder and S. J. Lopez (Eds.), *Oxford handbook of positive psychology* (pp. 393–403). New York, NY: Oxford University.

Cheng, C. Y., and Lee, F. (2009). Multiracial identity integration: Perceptions of conflict and distance among multiracial individuals. *Journal of Social Issues, 65*, 51–68.

Cialdini, R. B., and Trost, M. R. (1998). Social influence: Social norms, conformity, and compliance. In D. T. Gilbert, S. T. Fiske, and G. Lindzey (Eds.), *The handbook of social psychology*, Vol. 2, 4th ed. (pp. 151–92). Boston, MA: McGraw-Hill.

Clark, M. S., and Lemay, E. P. (2010). Close relationships. In S. T. Fiske, D. T. Gilbert, and G. Lindzey (Eds.), *The handbook of social psychology*, Vol. 2, 5th ed. (pp. 898–940). Hoboken, NJ: John Wiley & Sons.

Cochran, S. D. (2001). Emerging issues in research on lesbians' and gay men's mental health: Does sexual orientation really matter? *American Psychologist, 56*, 931–47.

Cohler, B. J., Hostetler, A. J., and Boxer, A. M. (1998). Generativity, social context, and lived experience: Narratives of gay men in middle adulthood. In D. P. McAdams and E. de St. Aubin (Eds.), *Generativity and adult development: How and why we care for the next generation.* (pp. 265–309). Washington, D.C.: American Psychological Association.

Constantine, M. G., and Sue, D. W. (2006). Factors contributing to optimal human functioning in people of color in the United States. *The Counseling Psychologist, 34*, 228–44.

Dahlsgaard, K., Peterson, C., and Seligman, M. E. P. (2005). Shared virtue: The convergence of valued human strengths across culture and history. *Review of General Psychology, 9*, 203–13.

Davidson, R. J., and Harrington, A. (Eds.) (2002). *Visions of compassion: Western scientists and Tibetan Buddhists examine human nature.* New York, NY: Oxford.

Deci, E. L., and Ryan, R. M. (2000). The "what" and "why" of goal pursuit: Human needs and the self-determination of behavior. *Psychological Inquiry, 11*, 227–68.

DeMaris, A. (2007). The role of relationship inequity in marital disruption. *Journal of Social and Personal Relationships, 24*, 177–95.

de Vries, B., and Megathlin, D. (2009). The meaning of friendship for gay men and lesbians in the second half of life. *Journal of GLBT Family Studies, 5*(1/2), 82–98.

Diamond, L. M. (2008). *Sexual fluidity: Understanding women's love and desire.* Cambridge, MA: Harvard University.

Diener, E. (2000). Subjective well-being: The science of happiness and a proposal for a national index. *American Psychologist, 55*, 34–43.

Diener, E., and Seligman, M. E. P. (2002). Very happy people. *Psychological Science, 13*, 81–84.

Dillon, C. (1999). A relational perspective on mutuality and boundaries in clinical practice with lesbians. In J. Baird (Ed.), *Lesbians and lesbian families: Reflections on theory & practice* (pp. 283–303). New York, NY: Columbia University.

Dudley, M. J., Rostosky, S. S., Riggle, E. D. B., Duhigg, J., Brodnicki, C., and Couch, R. (2005). Same-sex couples' experiences with homonegativity. *Journal of GLBT Family Studies, 1*(4), 68–93.

Duhigg, J. M., Rostosky, S. S., Gray, B. E., and Wimsatt, M. K. (2010). Development of heterosexuals into sexual-minority allies: A qualitative exploration. *Sexuality Research and Social Policy, 7*, 2–14.

Eliason, M. J., and Morgan, K. S. (1998). Lesbians define themselves: Diversity in lesbian identification. *Journal of Gay, Lesbian, and Bisexual Identity, 3,* 47–63.

Erich, S., Tittsworth, J., Dykes, J., and Cabuses, C. (2008). Family relationships and their correlations with transsexual well-being. *Journal of GLBT Family Studies, 4*(4), 419–32.

Erich, S., Tittsworth, J., and Kersten, A. S. (2010). An examination and comparison of transsexuals of color and their white counterparts regarding personal well-being and support networks. *Journal of GLBT Family Studies, 6*(1), 25–39.

Erikson, E. H. (1980). *Identity and the life cycle.* New York, NY: Norton.

Erikson, E. H. (1982). *The life cycle completed.* New York, NY: Norton.

Esmail, A. (2010). "Negotiating fairness": A study on how lesbian family members evaluate, construct, and maintain "fairness" with the division of household labor. *Journal of Homosexuality, 57*(5), 591–609.

Fassinger, R. E. (1998). Lesbian, gay, and bisexual identity and student development theory. In R. L. Sanlo (Ed.), *Working with lesbian, gay, bisexual, and transgender college students: A handbook for faculty and administrators* (pp. 13–22). Westport, CT: Greenwood Press.

Fassinger, R. E., and Arseneau, J. R. (2007). "I'd rather get wet than be under that umbrella": Differentiating the experiences and identities of lesbian, gay, bisexual, and transgender people. In K. J. Bieschke, R. M. Perez, and K. A. DeBord (Eds.) *Handbook of counseling and psychotherapy with lesbian, gay, bisexual, and transgender clients* (pp. 19–49). Washington, D.C.: American Psychological Association.

Fassinger, R. E., Shullman, S. L., and Stevenson, M. R. (2010). Toward an affirmative lesbian, gay, bisexual, and transgender leadership paradigm. *American Psychologist, 65*(3), 201–15.

Fausto-Sterling, A. (2000a). *Sexing the body: Gender politics and the construction of sexuality.* New York, NY: Basic Books.

Fausto-Sterling, A. (2000b). The five sexes, revisited. *The Sciences,* July/August, 18–23.

Fingerhut, A. W., Peplau, L. A., and Ghavami, N. (2005). A dual identity framework for understanding lesbian experience. *Psychology of Women Quarterly, 29*(2), 129–39.

Fingerhut, A. W., Riggle, E. D. B., and Rostosky, S. S. (2011). Marriage amendments and the same-sex marriage debate: The social, psychological, and policy implications. *Journal of Social Issues 67*(2), 225–41.

Finnegan, D. G., and McNally, E. B. (2002). *Counseling lesbian, gay, bisexual, and transgender substance abusers.* New York, NY: Haworth.

Firestein, B. A. (2007). Cultural and relational contexts of bisexual women: Implications for therapy. In K. J. Bieschke, R. M. Perez, and K. A. DeBord (Eds.) *Handbook of counseling and psychotherapy with lesbian, gay, bisexual, and transgender clients* (pp. 91–118). Washington, D.C.: American Psychological Association.

Fredrickson, B. L., Cohn, M. A., Coffey, K. A., Pek, J., and Finkel, S. M. (2008). Open hearts build lives: Positive emotions, induced through loving-kindness meditation, build consequential personal resources. *Journal of Personality and Social Psychology, 95*(5), 1045–62.

Friend, R. A. (1987). The individual and social psychology of aging: Clinical implications for lesbians and gay men. *Journal of Homosexuality, 14*, 307–31.

Friend, R. A. (1990). Older lesbian and gay people: A theory of successful aging. *Journal of Homosexuality, 20*, 99–118.

Frisch, M. B. (2006). *Quality of life therapy: Applying a life satisfaction approach to positive psychology and cognitive therapy.* New York, NY: John Wiley & Sons.

Galliher, R. V., Rostosky, S. S., and Hughes, H. K. (2004). School belonging, self-esteem, and depressive symptoms in adolescents: An examination of sex, sexual attraction status, and urbanicity. *Journal of Youth and Adolescence, 33*(3), 235–45.

Gambone, P. (2010). *Travels in a gay nation: Portraits of LGBTQ Americans.* Madison, WI: University of Wisconsin.

Gates, G. J., Badgett, M. V. L., Macomer, J. E., and Chambers, K. (2007). *Adoption and foster care by gay and lesbian parents in the United States.* Los Angeles, CA: The Williams Institute. Retrieved on Feb 10, 2011, from http://www2.law.ucla.edu/williamsinstitute/publications/FinalAdoptionReport.pdf.

Gilley, B. J. (2006). *Becoming Two-Spirit: Gay identity and social acceptance in Indian Country.* Lincoln, NE: University of Nebraska.

Godfrey, K., Haddock, S. A., Fisher, A., and Lund, L. (2006). Essential components of curricula for preparing therapists to work effectively with lesbian, gay, and bisexual clients: A delphi study. *Journal of Marital and Family Therapy, 32*, 491–504.

Goldberg, A. E. (2009). *Lesbian and gay parents and their children: Research on the family life cycle* (Contemporary Perspectives on Lesbian, Gay, and Bisexual Psychology). Washington, D.C.: American Psychological Association.

Goleman, D. (1997). *Emotional intelligence: Why it can matter more than IQ.* New York, NY: Bantam Books.

Goleman, D. (2006). *Social intelligence: The new science of human relationships.* New York, NY: Bantam Books.

Gomillion, S. C., and Giuliano, T. A. (2011). The influence of media role models on gay, lesbian, and bisexual identity. *Journal of Homosexuality, 58*(3), 330–54.

Gottman, J. M., Levenson, R. W., Gross, J., Fredrickson, B. L., McCoy, K., Rosenthal, L., Ruef, A., and Yoshimoto, D. (2003). Correlates of gay and lesbian couples' relationship satisfaction and relationship dissolution. *Journal of Homosexuality, 45*(1), 23–43.

Grant, J. M., Mottet, L. A., Tanis, J., Harrison, J., Herman, J. L., and Keisling, M. (2011). *Injustice at every turn: A report of the National Transgender Discrimination Survey.* Washington, D.C.: National Center for Transgender Equality and National Gay and Lesbian Task Force.

Greenfield, J. (2008). Coming out: The process of forming a positive identity. In H. J. Makadon, K. H. Mayer, J. Potter, and H. Goldhammer (Eds.) *The Fenway guide to lesbian, gay, bisexual, and transgender health* (pp. 45–74). Philadelphia, PA: American College of Physicians.

Haldeman, D. C. (2007). The village people: Identity and development in the gay male community. In K. J. Bieschke, R. M. Perez, and K. A. DeBord (Eds.) *Handbook of* counseling and psychotherapy with lesbian, gay, bisexual, and transgender clients (pp. 71–90). Washington, D.C.: American Psychological Association

Hall, D. M. (2009). *Allies at work: Creating a lesbian, gay, bisexual and transgender inclusive work environment*. San Francisco, CA: Out & Equal Workplace Advocates.

Harper, G. W., and Schneider, M. (2003). Oppression and discrimination among lesbian, gay, bisexual, and transgendered people and communities: A challenge for community psychology. *American Journal of Community Psychology, 31,* 243–52.

Harter, S. (2005). Authenticity. In Snyder, C. R., and Lopez, S. J. (Eds.), *Handbook of positive psychology* (pp. 382–94). New York, NY: Oxford University.

Heatherington, L., and Lavner, J. A. (2008). Coming to terms with coming out: Review and recommendations for family systems–focused research. *Journal of Family Psychology, 22*(3), 329–43.

Helminiak, D. (2008). *Spirituality for our global community: Beyond traditional religion to a world at peace.* Lanham, MD: Rowman & Littlefield.

Helms, H. M., Proulx, C. M., Klute, M. M., McHale, S. M, and Crouter, A. C. (2006). Spouses' gender-typed attributes and their links with marital quality: A pattern analytic approach. *Journal of Social and Personal Relationships, 23,* 843–64.

Helson, R., and Roberts, B. W. (1994). Ego development and personality change in adulthood. *Journal of Personality and Social Psychology, 66,* 911–20.

Hendrick, C., and Hendrick, S. S. (2000). *Close relationships: A sourcebook.* Thousand Oaks, CA: Sage.

Hendrick, C., and Hendrick, S. S. (2009). Love. In C. R. Snyder and S. J. Lopez (Eds.), *Oxford handbook of positive psychology* (pp. 447-454). New York, NY: Oxford University.

Hill, C. E. (Ed.). (2004). *Dream work in therapy: Facilitating exploration, insight, and action.* Washington, D.C.: American Psychological Association.

Hines, S. (2007). *TransForming gender: Transgender practices of identity and intimacy.* Bristol, UK: Policy Press.

Hines, S. (2010). Introduction. In S. Hines and T. Sanger (Eds.), *Transgender identities: Towards a social analysis of gender diversity* (pp. 1–22). New York, NY: Taylor & Francis.

Horne, S. G., Rostosky, S. S., and Riggle, E. D. B. (2011). Marriage restriction amendments and family members of lesbian, gay, and bisexual individuals: A mixed-method approach. *Journal of Social Issues* 67(2), 358–75.

Huffman, A. H., Watrous-Rodriguez, K. M., and King, E. B. (2008). Supporting a diverse workforce: What type of support is most meaningful for lesbian and gay employees? *Human Resource Management, 47*(2), 237–53.

Hutcherson, C. A., Seppala, E. M., and Gross, J. J. (2008). Loving-kindness meditation increases social connectedness. *Emotion, 8*(5), 720–24.

Imber-Black, E. (2003). Ritual themes in families and family therapy. In E. Imber-Black, J. Roberts, and R. Whiting (Eds.), *Rituals in families and family therapy* (2nd ed., pp. 49–87). New York, NY: Norton.

Ivey, A. E., Ivey, M. B., and Zalaquett, C. P. (2010). *Intentional interviewing and counseling: Facilitating client development in a multicultural society.* Belmont, CA: Brooks/Cole.

Jacobs, S. E., Wesley, T., and Lang, S. (1997). Introduction. In S. E. Jacobs, W. Thomas, and S. Lang (eds.), *Two-Spirit People: Native American gender identity, sexuality and spirituality* (pp. 1–20). Chicago, IL: University of Illinois Press.

Johnson, F. (2003). *Keeping the faith: A skeptic's journey among Christian and Buddhist monks.* New York: NY: Houghton Mifflin.

Kashdan, T. B., and Silvia, P. J. (2009). Curiosity and interest: The benefits of thriving on novelty and challenge. In C. R. Snyder and S. J. Lopez (Eds.), *Oxford handbook of positive psychology* (pp. 367–74). New York, NY: Oxford University.

Kaufman, R. (2008). Introduction to transgender identity and health. In H. J. Makadon, K. H. Mayer, J. Potter, and H. Goldhammer (Eds.), *The Fenway guide to lesbian, gay, bisexual, and transgender health.* Philadelphia, PA: American College of Physicians.

King, C. R., Bloodsworth-Lugo, M. K., and Lugo-Lugo, C. R. (2010). *Animating difference: Race, gender, and sexuality in contemporary films for children.* Lanham, MD: Rowman & Littlefield.

King, L. A. (2001). The hard road to the good life: The happy, mature person. *Journal of Humanistic Psychology, 41,* 51–72.

King, L. A. (2008). Interventions for enhancing subjective well-being: Can we make people happier and should we? In M. Eid and R. J. Larsen (Eds.), *The science of subjective well-being.* (pp. 431–48). New York, NY: Guilford.

King, L. A., Burton, C. M., and Geise, A. C. (2009). The good (gay) life: The search for signs of maturity in the narratives of gay adults. In P. L. Hammack and B. J. Cohler (Eds.), *The story of sexual identity: Narrative perspectives on the gay and lesbian life course* (pp. 375–96). New York, NY: Oxford University.

Kurdek, L. A. (2004). Are gay and lesbian cohabiting couples really different from heterosexual married couples? *Journal of Marriage and Family, 66,* 880–900.

Kurdek, L. A. (2005). What do we know about gay and lesbian couples? *Current Directions in Psychological Science, 14*(5), 251–54.

Kurdek, L. A. (2006). Differences between partners from heterosexual, gay, and lesbian cohabiting couples. *Journal of Marriage and Family, 68*(2), 509–28.

Kurdek, L. A. (2008). Change in relationship quality for partners from lesbian, gay male, and heterosexual couples. *Journal of Family Psychology, 22,* 701–11.

Laboy, M. M., Sandfort, T., and Yi, H. (2009). Global perspectives on same-sex sexualities: Desires, practices, and identities. *Sexuality Research and Social Policy, 6*(2–3), 1–3.

Leary, M. R. (2008). Affiliation, acceptance, and belonging: The pursuit of interpersonal connection. In S. T. Fiske, D. T. Gilbert, and G. Lindzey (Eds.) *Handbook of social psychology* (5th ed.) (pp. 864–97). New York, NY: John Wiley & Sons.

Lease, S. H., Horne, S. G., and Noffsinger-Frazier, N. (2005). Affirming faith experiences and psychological health for Caucasian lesbian, gay, and bisexual individuals. *Journal of Counseling Psychology, 52*(3), 378–88.

LeBeau, R. T., and Jellison, W. A. (2009). Why get involved? Exploring gay and bisexual men's experience of the gay community. *Journal of Homosexuality, 56*(1), 56–76.

Lechner, S. C., Tennen, H., and Affleck, G. (2009). Benefit-finding and growth. In C. R. Snyder and S. J. Lopez (Eds.), *Oxford handbook of positive psychology* (pp. 633–40). New York, NY: Oxford University.

Lefcourt, H. M. (2005). Humor. In C. R. Snyder and S. J. Lopez (Eds.), *Handbook of positive psychology* (pp. 619–31). New York, NY: Oxford University.

Lehavot, K., Balsam, K. F., and Ibrahim-Wells, G. D. (2009). Redefining the American quilt: Definitions and experiences of community among ethnically diverse lesbian and bisexual women. *Journal of Community Psychology, 37*(4), 439–58.

Lemish, D. (2008). Gender representations in the media. In *International encyclopedia of communication* (Vol. V) (pp. 1945–51). Oxford, UK: Blackwell Publishing.

Lev, A. I. (2004). *Transgender emergence: Therapeutic guidelines for working with gender variant people and their families.* Binghamton, NY: Haworth Clinical Practice Press.

Lev, A. I. (2007). Transgender communities: Developing identity through connection. In K. J. Bieschke, R. M. Perez, and K. A. DeBord (Eds.), *Handbook of counseling and psychotherapy with lesbian, gay, bisexual, and transgender clients* (2nd ed.) (pp. 147–75). Washington, D.C.: American Psychological Association.

Levant, R. F., and Richmond, K. (2007). A review of research on masculinity ideologies using the male role norms inventory. *Journal of Men's Studies, 15,* 130–46.

Liddle, B. J. (1996). Therapist sexual orientation, gender, and counseling practices as they relate to ratings of helpfulness by gay and lesbian clients. *Journal of Counseling Psychology, 43,* 394–401.

Liddle, B. J. (2007). Mutual bonds: Lesbian women's lives and communities. In K. J. Bieschke, R. M. Perez, and K. A. DeBord (Eds.), *Handbook of counseling and psychotherapy with lesbian, gay, bisexual, and transgender clients* (pp. 51–70). Washington, D.C.: American Psychological Association.

Loevinger, J. (1976). *Ego development: Conceptions and theories.* San Francisco, CA: Jossey-Bass.

Lynn, M., and Snyder, C. R. (2005). Uniqueness seeking. In C. R. Snyder and S. J. Lopez (Eds.), *Handbook of positive psychology* (pp. 395–410). New York, NY: Oxford University.

Mackey, R. A., Diemer M. A., and O'Brien, B. A. (2004). Relational factors in understanding satisfaction in the lasting relationships of same-sex and heterosexual couples. *Journal of Homosexuality, 47,* 111–36.

Maisel, N. C., and Gable, S. L. (2009). For richer . . . in good times . . . and in health: Positive processes in relationships. In C. R. Snyder and S. J. Lopez (Eds.), *Oxford handbook of positive psychology* (pp. 455–62). New York, NY: Oxford University.

Maguen, S., Shipherd, J. C., Harris, H. N., and Welch, L. P. (2007). Prevalence and predictors of disclosure of transgender identity. *International Journal of Sexual Health, 19,* 3–13.

Makadon, H. J., Mayer, K. H., Potter, J., and Goldhammer, H. (Eds.) (2007). *Fenway guide to lesbian, gay, bisexual & transgender health.* Philadelphia, PA: American College of Physicians.

McAdams, D. P., Diamond, A., de St. Aubin, E., and Mansfield, E. (1997). Stories of commitment: The psychosocial construction of generative lives. *Journal of Personality and Social Psychology, 72*(3), 678–94.

McLelland, M., Suganuma, K., and Welker, J. (2007). *Queer voices from Japan: First person narratives from Japan's sexual minorities*. Lanham, MD: Lexington Books.

Mejía, X. E. (2005). Gender matters: Working with adult male survivors of trauma. *Journal of Counseling & Development, 83*(1), 29–40.

Meyer, I. H. (2003). Prejudice, social stress, and mental health in lesbian, gay, and bisexual populations: Conceptual issues and research evidence. *Psychological Bulletin, 129*, 674–97.

Meyer, I. H., and Northridge, M. E. (2007). *The health of sexual minorities: Public health perspectives on lesbian, gay, bisexual and transgender populations*. New York, NY: Springer.

Miller, J. B., and Stiver, I. (1991). What do we mean by relationships? In *Works in Progress, 52*. Wellesley, MA: Stone Center Working Paper Series.

Moorhead, C. (1999). Queering identities: The roles of integrity and belonging in becoming ourselves. *Journal of Gay, Lesbian, and Bisexual Identity, 4*(4), 327–43.

Nakamura, J., and Csikszentmihalyi, M. (2003). The construction of meaning through vital engagement. In C. L. M. Keyes and J. Haidt (Eds.), *Flourishing: Positive psychology and the life well-lived* (pp. 83–104). Washington, D.C.: American Psychological Association.

Nestle, J., Wilchins, R., and Howell, C. (2002). *GenderQueer: Voices from beyond the sexual binary*. New York, NY: Alyson Books.

Ochs, R., and Rowley, S. E. (2009). *Getting bi: Voices of bisexual around the world* (2nd ed.). Boston, MA: Bisexual Resource Center.

O'Connell, A. (1999). Voices from the heart: The developmental impact of a mother's lesbianism on her adolescent children. In J. Laird (Ed.), *Lesbians and lesbian families: Reflections on theory and practice* (pp. 261–80). New York, NY: Columbia University.

Oswald, R. F. (2002). Resilience with the family networks of lesbians and gay men: Intentionality and redefinition. *Journal of Marriage & Family, 64*, 374–83.

Otis, M. D., Rostosky, S. S., Riggle, E. D. B., and Hamrin, R. (2006). Stress and relationship quality in same-sex couples. *Journal of Social and Personal Relationships, 23*(1), 81–99.

Page, E. (2007). Bisexual women's and men's experiences of psychotherapy. In B. A. Firestein (Ed.) *Becoming visible: Counseling bisexuals across the lifespan* (pp. 52–71). New York, NY: Columbia University.

Palmer, P. (1998). *The courage to teach: Exploring the inner landscape of a teacher's life*. San Francisco, CA: Jossey-Bass.

Park, N., Peterson, C., and Seligman, M. E. P. (2004). Strengths of character and well-being. *Journal of Social and Clinical Psychology, 23*(5), 603–19.

Park, N., Peterson, C., and Seligman, M. E. P. (2006). Character strengths in fifty-four nations and the fifty US states. *The Journal of Positive Psychology, 1*(3), 118–29.

Peplau, L. A., and Fingerhut, A. W. (2007). The close relationships of lesbians and gay men. *Annual Review of Psychology, 58*, 405–24.

Peterson, C., and Chang, E. C. (2003). Optimism and flourishing. In C. L. M. Keyes and J. Haidt (Eds.), *Flourishing: Positive psychology and the life well-lived* (pp. 55–79). Washington, D.C.: American Psychological Association.

Peterson, C., and Seligman, M. E. P. (2004). *Character strengths and virtues: A handbook and classification*. New York, NY: Oxford University.

Potoczniak, D. J. (2007). Development of bisexual men's identities and relationships. In K. J. Bieschke, R. M. Perez, and K. A. DeBord (Eds.) *Handbook of counseling and psychotherapy with lesbian, gay, bisexual, and transgender clients* (pp. 119–46). Washington, D.C.: American Psychological Association.

Pury, C. L. S., and Lopez, S. J. (2009). Courage. In C. R. Snyder and S. J. Lopez (Eds.), *Oxford handbook of positive psychology* (pp. 375–82). New York, NY: Oxford University.

Remer, P., and Remer, R. (2000). The alien invasion exercise: An experience of diversity. *International Journal of Action Methods: Psychodrama, Skill Training, and Role-Playing*, 52, 147–54.

Rich, A. (1980). Compulsory heterosexuality and lesbian existence. *Signs*, 5, 631–60.

Riggle, E. D. B., and Rostosky, S. S. (2005). For better or worse: Psycholegal soft spots and advance planning for same-sex couples. *Professional Psychology: Research and Practice*, 35, 90–96.

Riggle, E. D. B., Rostosky, S. S., Couch, R., Brodnicki, C., Campbell, J., and Savage, T. (2006). To have or not to have: Advance planning by same-sex couples. *Sexuality Research and Social Policy*, 3, 22–32.

Riggle, E. D. B., Rostosky, S. S., and Horne, S. G. (2009). Marriage amendments and lesbian, gay, and bisexual individuals in the 2006 election. *Sexuality Research and Social Policy*, 6, 80–89.

Riggle, E. D. B., Rostosky, S. S., and Horne, S. G. (2010a). Psychological distress, well-being, and legal recognition in same-sex couple relationships. *Journal of Family Psychology*, 24, 82–86.

Riggle, E. D. B., Rostosky, S. S., and Horne, S. G. (2010b). Does it matter where you live? State non-discrimination laws and the perceptions of LGB residents. *Sexuality Research and Social Policy*, 7, 168–72.

Riggle, E. D. B., Rostosky, S. S., McCants, L. E., and Pascal-Hague, D. (2011). The positive aspects of a transgender self-identification. *Psychology & Sexuality*, 2, 1–12.

Riggle, E. D. B., Rostosky, S. S., and Prather, R. A. (2006). The execution of advance planning documents by same-sex couples. *Journal of Family Issues*, 27, 758–76.

Riggle, E. D. B., Thomas, J. D., and Rostosky, S. S. (2005). The marriage debate and minority stress. *PS: Political Science and Politics*, 38, 21–24.

Riggle, E. D. B., Whitman, J., Olson, A., Rostosky, S. S., and Strong, S. (2008). The positive aspects of being a lesbian or gay man. *Professional Psychology: Research and Practice*, 39, 210–17.

Ritter, K. Y., and Terndrup, A. I. (2002). *Handbook of affirmative psychotherapy with lesbians and gay men*. New York, NY: Guilford.

Robb, C. (2006). *This changes everything: The relational revolution in psychology*. New York, NY: Farrar, Straus and Giroux.

Rogers, C. (1977). *On becoming a person: A therapist's view of psychotherapy*. London, England: Constable and Robinson.

Roisman, G. I., Clausell, E., Holland, A., Fortuna, K., and Elief, C. (2008). Adult romantic relationships as contexts for human development: A multimethod comparison of same-sex couples with opposite-sex dating, engaged and married dyads. *Developmental Psychology, 44*, 91–101.

Roscoe, W. (1998). *Changing ones: Third and fourth genders in Native North America.* New York, NY: St. Martin's Press.

Rosenblum, K. E., and Travis, T. C. (2008). *The meaning of difference: American constructions of race, sex and gender, social class, sexual orientation, and disability* (5th ed.). New York, NY: McGraw-Hill.

Rostosky, S. S., Korfhage, B., Duhigg, J., Stern, A., Bennett, L., and Riggle, E. D. B. (2004). Same-sex couples' perceptions of family support: A consensual qualitative study. *Family Process, 43*, 43–56.

Rostosky, S. S., Otis, M. D., Riggle, E. D. B., Kelley, S., and Brodnicki, C. (2007). An exploratory study of religiosity and same-sex couple relationships. *Journal of GLBT Family Studies, 3*, 17–36.

Rostosky, S. S., Owens, G. P., Zimmerman, R. S., and Riggle, E. D. B. (2003). Associations among sexual attraction status, school belonging, and alcohol and marijuana use in rural high school students. *Journal of Adolescence, 26*(6), 741–51.

Rostosky, S. S., and Riggle, E. D. B. (2002). Out at work: The relation of actor and partner workplace policy and internalized homophobia to disclosure status. *Journal of Counseling Psychology, 49*, 411–19.

Rostosky, S. S., Riggle, E. D. B., Brodnicki, C., and Olson, A. (2009). An exploration of lived religion in same-sex couples from Judeo-Christian religions. *Family Process, 47*, 389–403.

Rostosky, S. S., Riggle, E. D. B., Dudley, M. G., and Comer Wright, M. L. (2006). Relational commitment: A qualitative analysis of same-sex couples' conversations. *Journal of Homosexuality, 51*, 199–223.

Rostosky, S. S., Riggle, E. D. B., Gray, B. E., and Hatton, R. L. (2007). Minority stress experiences in committed same-sex couple relationships. *Professional Psychology: Research and Practice, 38*, 392–400.

Rostosky, S. S., Riggle, E. D. B., Horne, S. G., and Miller, A. D. (2009). Marriage amendments and psychological distress in lesbian, gay and bisexual (LGB) adults. *Journal of Counseling Psychology, 56*, 56–66.

Rostosky, S. S., Riggle, E. D. B., Horne, S.G., Denton, F. N., and Huellemeier, J. D. (2010). Lesbian, gay, and bisexual individuals' psychological reactions to amendments denying access to civil marriage. *American Journal of Orthopsychiatry, 80*, 302–10.

Rostosky, S. S., Riggle, E. D. B., Pascal-Hague, D., and McCants, L. E. (2010). The positive aspects of a bisexual self-identification. *Psychology & Sexuality, 1*, 131–44.

Rostosky, S. S., Riggle, E. D. B., Savage, T., Couch, J. R., Roberts, S. D., and Singletary, G. (2008). Interracial same-sex couples' perceptions of stress and coping: An exploratory study. *Journal of GLBT Family Studies, 4*, 1–23.

Rothblum, E. D. (2009). An overview of same-sex couples in relationships: A research area still at sea. In D. A. Hope (Ed.), *Contemporary perspectives on lesbian, gay, and bisexual identities* (pp. 113–39). New York, NY: Springer.

Rothblum, E. D. (2010). Where is the "women's community"? Voices of lesbian, bisexual and queer women and their heterosexual sisters. *Feminism & Psychology, 20,* 454–72.

Rubin, G. (2006). "Of catamites and kings: Reflections on butch, gender, and boundaries." In S. Stryker and S. Whittle (Eds.), *The transgender studies reader* (pp. 471–81). New York, NY: Routledge.

Rumens, N. (2010). Firm friends: Exploring the supportive components in gay men's workplace friendships. *The Sociological Review, 58*(1), 135–55.

Russell, G. M., and Horne, S. G. (2009). Finding equilibrium: Mentoring, sexual orientation, and gender identity. *Professional Psychology: Research and Practice, 40*(2), 194–200.

Russell, G. M., and Richards, J. A. (2003). Stressor and resilience factors for lesbians, gay men, and bisexuals confronting antigay politics. *American Journal of Community Psychology, 31*(3–4), 313–28.

Russell, S. T., Muraco, A., Subramaniam, A., and Laub, C. (2009). Youth empowerment and high school Gay-Straight Alliances. *Journal of Youth and Adolescence, 38*(7), 891–903.

Rust, P. C. R. (2002). Bisexuality: The state of the union. *Annual Review of Sex Research, 13,* 180–240.

Ryff, C., and Keyes, C. (1995). The structure of psychological well-being revisited. *Journal of Personality and Social Psychology, 69,* 719–27.

Ryff, C. D. (1989). Happiness is everything, or is it? Explorations on the meaning of psychological well-being. *Journal of Personality and Social Psychology, 57*(6), 1069–81.

Salovey, P., Mayer, J. D., Caruso, D., and Yoo, S. H. (2009). The positive psychology of emotional intelligence. In C. R. Snyder and S. J. Lopez (Eds.), *Oxford handbook of positive psychology* (pp. 237–48). New York, NY: Oxford University.

Sang, B. E. (1993). Existential issues of midlife lesbians. In L. D. Garnets and D. C. Kimmel (Eds.), *Psychological perspectives on lesbian and gay male experiences* (pp. 500–16) New York, NY: Columbia University.

Sanger, T. (2008). Queer(y)ing gender and sexuality: Transpeople's lived experiences and intimate partnerships. In L. Moon (Ed.), *Feeling queer or queer feelings?: Radical approaches to counselling sex, sexualities and genders* (pp. 72–88). New York, NY: Routledge.

Savage, D., and Miller, T. (Eds.) (2010). *It gets better: Coming out, overcoming bullying, and creating a life worth living.* New York, NY: Dutton.

Scharrer, E., Kim, D. D., Lin, K. M., and Liu, Z. (2006). Working hard or hardly working? Gender, humor, and the performance of domestic chores in television commercials. *Mass Communication & Society, 9*(2), 215–38.

Scherrer, K. S. (2010). The intergenerational and family relationships of grandparents and GLBQ grandchildren. *Journal of GLBT Family Studies, 6,* 229–64.

Seligman, M. E. P. (2002). *Authentic happiness*. New York, NY: Free Press.

Seligman, M. E. P., Steen, T. A., Park, N., and Peterson, C. (2005). Positive psychology progress: Empirical validation of interventions. *American Psychologist, 60*(5), 410–21.

Simon, R. J., and Brooks, A. M. (2009). *Gay and lesbian communities the world over*. Lanham, MD: Lexington Books.

Simonsen, G., Blazina, C., and Watkins, C. E. (2000). Gender role conflict and psychological well-being among gay men. *Journal of Counseling Psychology, 47*(1), 85–89.

Solomon, S. E, Rothblum E. D., and Balsam, K. F. (2004). Pioneers in the partnership: Lesbian and gay male couples compared with those not in civil unions, and married heterosexual siblings. *Journal of Family Psychology, 18*, 275–86.

Solomon, S. E, Rothblum, E. D., and Balsam, K. F. (2005). Money, housework, sex, and conflict: Same-sex couples in civil unions, those not in civil unions, and heterosexual siblings. *Sex Roles, 52*, 561–75.

Steffen, P. R., and Masters, K. S. (2005). Does compassion mediate the intrinsic relation-health relationship? *Annals of Behavioral Medicine, 30*, 217–24.

Steger, M. F. (2009). Meaning in life. In C. R. Snyder and S. J. Lopez (Eds.), *Oxford handbook of positive psychology* (pp. 679–87). New York, NY: Oxford University.

Stone, D. (2008). Wounded healing: Exploring the circle of compassion in the helping relationship. *The Humanistic Psychologist, 36*, 45–51.

Sue, D. W., and Constantine, M. G. (2003). Optimal human functioning in people of color in the United States. In Walsh, B. (Ed.) *Counseling psychology and optimal human functioning* (pp. 151–70). Mahwah, NJ: Lawrence Erlbaum Associates.

Swann, W. B., and Bosson, J. K. (2010). Self and identity. In S. T. Fiske, D. T. Gilbert, and G. Lindzey (Eds.), *The handbook of social psychology*, Vol. 1, 5th ed. (pp. 589–628). Hoboken, NJ: John Wiley & Sons.

Swearer, S. M., Espelage, D. L., and Napolitano, S. A. (2009). *Bullying prevention and intervention: Realistic strategies for schools*. New York, NY: Guilford.

Swigonski, M. (1995). Claiming a lesbian identity as an act of empowerment. *Affilia, 19*(4), 413–25.

Thorndike, E. L. (2007). *Human intelligence*. Bloomington, IN: Indiana University. Retrieved from http://www.indiana.edu/~intell/ethorndike.shtml.

Tulgade, M. M., and Fredrickson, B. L. (2007). Regulation of positive emotions: Emotion regulation strategies that promote resilience. *Journal of Happiness Studies, 8*, 311–33.

Van Keelf, G. A., Oveis, C., van der Lowe, I., LuoKogan, A., Goetz, J., and Keltner, D. (2008). Power, distress, and compassion: Turning a blind eye to the suffering of others. *Psychological Science, 19*, 1315–22.

Wachholtz, A. B., and Pearce, M. (2007). Compassion and health. In T. G. Plante and C. E. Thoresen (Eds.), *Spirit, science, and health: How the spiritual mind fuels physical wellness* (pp. 115–28). Westport, CT: Praeger.

Waterman, A. S. (1993). Two conceptions of happiness: Contrast of personal expressiveness (eudaimonia) and hedonic enjoyment. *Journal of Personality and Social Psychology, 64*, 678–91.

Watson, D., and Naragon, K. (2009). Positive affectivity: The disposition to experience positive emotional states. In C. R. Snyder and S. J. Lopez (Eds.), *Oxford handbook of positive psychology* (pp. 207–15). New York, NY: Oxford University.

Weston, K. (1991). *Families we choose*. New York, NY: Columbia University.

Wilson, B. D. M., and Miller, R. L. (2002). Strategies for managing heterosexism used among African American gay and bisexual men. *Journal of Black Psychology, 28*, 371–91.

Wood, J. T. (2010). *Interpersonal communication: Everyday encounters*. Belmont, CA: Wadsworth Cengage Learning.

Wood, W., and Eagly, A. H. (2010). Gender. In S. T. Fiske, D. T. Gilbert, and G. Lindzey (Eds.), *The handbook of social psychology*, Vol. 1, 5th ed. (pp. 629–67). Hoboken, NJ: John Wiley & Sons.

Worrell, J. (Ed.) (2001). *Encyclopedia of women and gender: Sex similarities and differences and the impact of society on gender*. San Diego, CA: Academic Press.

Zea, M. C., Reisen, C. A., and Poppen, P. J. (1999). Psychological well-being among Latino lesbians and gay men. *Cultural Diversity and Ethnic Minority Psychology, 5*(4), 371–79.

Zimmerman, M. A. (1995). Psychological empowerment: Issues and illustrations. *American Journal of Community Psychology, 23*(5), 581–99.

INDEX

ABOUT THE AUTHORS

Ellen D. B. Riggle, PhD, is a professor of gender and women's studies and political science at the University of Kentucky. She is cofounder of PrismResearch.org, a research group and website focused on issues impacting the well-being of LGBTQ individuals and same-sex couples. Her research investigates the impact of identity, legal status issues, and minority stress on the well-being of LGBTQ individuals and same-sex couples.

Sharon S. Rostosky, PhD, is a licensed psychologist and a professor of counseling psychology at the University of Kentucky. She is cofounder of PrismResearch.org. Her research interests focuses on the psychosocial well-being of LGBTQ individuals, same-sex couples, and their families.